100 cc
A Century of Communication

100 cc
A Century of Communication

Rajiv Soni

Rupa & Co

Copyright © Tata Steel Limited 2010

Published 2010 by
Rupa Publications India Pvt. Ltd.
7/16, Ansari Road, Daryaganj
New Delhi 110 002

Sales Centres:
Allahabad Bengaluru Chandigarh Chennai
Hyderabad Jaipur Kathmandu
Kolkata Mumbai

All rights reserved.
No part of this publication may be reproduced, stored in
a retrieval system, or transmitted, in any form or by any
means, electronic, mechanical, photocopying, recording or
otherwise, without the prior permission of the publishers.

Research & Design by
Avant Garde Omnimedia
16A Chowringhee Mansions
30 Jawaharlal Nehru Road
Kolkata 700 016
www.agomnimedia.com

Printed in India by
Nutech Photolithographers
B-240, Okhla Industrial Area, Phase-I
New Delhi 110 020, India

Preface

It was certainly the most patriotic of Indians, at the turn of the century, who believed that the vision carved for the company by its Founder also determined the future of the country. The inevitable cynics were silenced by the strong belief of these men who invested in the company and by the will of those who continued to work for the company when times were more than turbulent.

Their belief stemmed from the simple, honest yet strong messages from the company. From the earliest days, one of the biggest strengths of Tata Steel has been its transparency and credibility in its thoughts and transactions. To build a favourable image for a company is a challenge that has always daunted and tested the skills of communicators anywhere in the world. In the case of Tata Steel the challenge was to carve a niche in the emerging steel industry and at the same time to inject the spirit of patriotism in the citizens – a role that communicators of the company attempted and successfully achieved.
This was the genesis of Corporate Patriotism.

The Tata Iron and Steel Company, now Tata Steel Limited, was incorporated on the 26th of August, 1907, and its contribution to the growth and development of India since then is what other corporates can only aspire to do.

The idea of compiling a set of advertisements that would weave the history of the company through the last ten decades germinated a few years ago. At the same time the Tata Steel Archives had been established in Jamshedpur. Many of the advertisements reproduced in this book are from these Archives. Data and other material are taken from other sources which are mentioned in the References at the end of the book. There are no records, however, of any brief to the agencies and, as such, the comments in this book fringe on conjectures. This book does not attempt to be the history of advertising in India in the last hundred years and most certainly does not attempt to be an archive of all the advertisements released by Tata Steel.

Volumes have been written, by many eminent personalities, about the history of the company and the men who dared to dream and shape its future. I have neither the temerity nor the insight to rewrite their work. This publication simply salutes the vision and the creative thoughts of the communicators of the company who sought not only to build a great company but a better India.

I would like to thank Mr. B Muthuraman whose encouragement and inputs took this from a thought to fruition and Mr. H M Nerurkar for his time and guidance in going through the dummy copy.

This book would have also not been possible with out the encouragement that I have received from Tata Steel. I would especially like to mention Mr. Bimlendra Jha, Mr. Sanjiv Paul, Mr. Sanjay Choudhry and Ms. Madhulika Sharma for their constant support. A special mention of Ms. Gargi Gupta (the latter spent many hours to locate many of the advertisements in Tata Centre) and to the team at the Tata Steel Archives, Jamshedpur for their assistance.

I would also like to thank Mr. Samir Prasad of Avant Garde Omnimedia, and his team of Antara Ghosh, Tapan Samanta and Subha Rathee in the scanning of the archival material and in designing the publication and lastly Mr. Kapish Mehra, of Rupa & Company, who took one look at the dummy copy and said "When do we print?"

Foreword

The legacy of advertising at Tata Steel is as old as the Company itself. Ever since its inception over a hundred years ago, Tata Steel has leveraged advertising as a medium to get its message across to the masses. In the years before India gained its Independence, the messaging through advertising had less to do with the Company's products and more to do with sowing the seeds of industrialization in a country that was gripped with the fervour of patriotism.

Post the Second World War and in the early years of our Independence, the underlying theme of most advertisements issued by Tata Steel was on rebuilding the nation. With the advent of the Five Year Plans, the Company's advertisements were aimed at promoting increased use of steel that would facilitate all-round development and help lay the foundation of a richer and more prosperous India and its people.

Tata Steel has, over the years, used the advertisement route to pay tribute to the nation's Armed Forces, sportspersons and those who have dedicated their lives for the betterment of their country and countrymen. Advertisements have also been especially designed to commemorate milestones that were achieved as the years rolled by, such as development of special steels for defence applications or for the Railways. Few are aware that 85 per cent of the steel used to build Howrah Bridge was supplied by Tata Steel. The Company was among the first in the steel domain globally to brand steel as a commodity. Thus, for Tata Steel, the era of branding began in the early 1930s.

This book seeks to document some of the advertisements that were released by Tata Steel in the first 100 years of its existence. Advertisements that were fiercely nationalistic, those that raised the bar for industrialization in India, those that conveyed tongue-in-cheek messages, albeit subtly, et al. This book, aptly titled 100 CC (A Century of Communication) is bound to provide readers with a delightful insight into Tata Steel's Journey as an advertiser over the 100 years gone by.

H M Nerurkar
Managing Director
Tata Steel Limited

The Statesman 30 August 1907

THE TATA IRON SCHEME

FIRST MEETING OF THE COMPANY

BOMBAY, Aug. 28

The first meeting of the Tata Iron and Steel Company has been held, and the final prospectus passed. The subscription list will open on Thursday next, and close on the 14th of September. All ordinary shares, two hundred thousand in number, and 10,000 preference shares, have been taken up. The balance of 40,000 preference shares, and 2,000 deferred shares, will be offered to the public. The list will remain open till the 14th, particularly with a view of giving up country subscribers an opportunity to take up shares. In the final prospectus of the Company, the nominal capital is put down at two crores, thirty-one lakhs, and seventy-five thousand rupees, divided into three classes of shares, (1) two lakhs ordinary shares, of seventy-five rupees each; (2) fifty thousand preference shares of one hundred and fifty rupees each; (3) twenty-two thousand five hundred deferred shares of thirty rupees each. It is announced that it is the present intention to call up ordinary share capital to such an extent only as will make the total called-up capital of the Company approximately one and a half crore of rupees. Thus if the whole number of preference shares is taken up only about half the ordinary share capital will be called. Preference shares are to carry interest from 1st April, 1908. To allow of this being done, Messrs. Tata Sons and Company have agreed to transfer to the Company all their mineral concessions, which include the splendid manganese properties of Ramrama in the Central Provinces. Tatas are giving up their prospective profits from the manganese properties, to make the preference shares more popular upon terms to be hereafter arranged between the vendees and the directors.

THE TATA STEEL PROJECT.

The Tata Iron and Steel project has met with such approbation in India and there has been such a rush for shares that Messrs. Tata and Sons have decided to entertain no further applications for ordinary shares of their Iron and Steel Company. The 100,000 ordinary shares of Rs. 75 each have already been oversubscribed. There are a few preference shares still unsubscribed. The Company's capital is at present fixed at Rs. 1,53,00,000 divided as follows:—

1,00,000 shares of Rs. 75 each ... Rs. 75,00,000
50,000 cumulative 6 per cent preference shares of Rs. 150 each .... Rs. 75,00,000
10,000 deferred shares of Rs. 30 each .... Rs. 3,00,000

Total...... Rs. 1,53,00,000

This is, however, subject to alteration, and if it is thought desirable the capital of the Company may be increased. The unsolicited applications for shares amount to Rs. 1,60,00,000, and every day further subscriptions pour in. A meeting of the Board of Directors will be held when consideration will be given to a fresh prospectus and the Articles of Association of the Company will be passed. If the Directors decide to increase the capital it will not be called up. The Directors are: Sir Sassoon David, Sir Jehangir Cowasji Readymoney, Mr. Dorab J. Tata, Mr. Fazulbhoy Currimbhoy Ebrahim, Mr. Narotum Morarji Gokuldas, the Hon. Mr. Vithaldas D. Thackersey, Mr. Gordhandas Khatao Mukanji and Mr. Ardeshir J. Billimoria.

A report in The Statesman, Calcutta in September, 1907 highlighted the fact that the share issue for the Iron and Steel venture by the Tatas had been oversubscribed many times over and there was a decision by the company not to entertain any more applications. The news report added that the Management would meet to discuss if the capital needed to be increased.

The Share Issue

The proposal to set up the Iron and Steel plant near the small hamlet of Sakchi was near perfect. The ambitious venture had supreme viability with iron ore, coal and fluxes found in abundance not far away from the confluence of the two rivers of Kharkai and Subarnarekha. A railway line which connected Calcutta to Bombay was only a few kilometers away. The nearest sea-port was located 200 kilometers away. The combination of material and logistics could not have been more ideal for those times. In addition the Government provided all the encouragement and support.

Unfortunately the request for capital by the Tatas was regretted in London. The governing thoughts of the investors were influenced by the model and tradition of the East India Company which was not to put back anything into India. The investors also sought more control of the company which was not accepted by the Tata House. The project was deemed an Indian project to be run by Indians and thus did not evict a positive response.

Sir Dorab Tata, the eldest son of Tata Group founder J N Tata, boldly decided to test waters in India and explore the possibility of floating the steel company in Bombay (present day Mumbai) with Indian capital. It was the summer of 1907 and a new force was rising in the minds of Indian populace both rich and poor alike - this was the force of Swadeshi.

It was decided to issue a prospectus in Bombay to raise capital worth ₹ 23 million. This decision was met with skepticism by the British, predictably so, who felt that it was necessary to not only have English money to meet the capital requirement but also English brains to run the company!

The prospectus was issued in Bombay on 30th of August 1907 and was intended to close on the 14th of September the same year. For the next few days the rich combined with the working class crowded the Tata offices. The entire share capital was subscribed 'by 9000 people in eight days' which prompted the company not to entertain any further requests for ordinary shares.

The share holders came from every community in India. Apart from the Tata family and other Parsee merchants the other share holders were Gordhandas and Khattau, the Maharajas of Baroda, Mysore and Bhavnagar – all Hindus, FC Ibrahim, a Muslim merchant, M Hirachand, a Jain businessman, Mr. S David a Jewish Merchant and Mr. C S Clarke a British Banker. 15 Maharajas and Princes accounted for 13% of the share capital a 'good showing for a group much criticized for not having used its wealth to further India's economic growth.'

To quote from Keenan's - A Steel Man In India - *"It was now the summer of 1907 and a new powerful interior force was stirring the minds of the people of India, rich and poor alike, the Swadeshi movement. Swadeshi is roughly translated as "Produce your own goods". Sir Dorab boldly decided to test his India, to see if it was possible to float the steel company in Bombay with Indian capital. The Britishers in India were complacent. Now you will see, they said wisely, how necessary it is to have England at your back with her money and her brains. Indian capital, indeed! The prospectus was issued in Bombay on August 27, 1907. And all through the day the Tata office was besieged by Indians, a few of whom were obviously opulent, but many of whom were dressed in the worn garments of the poor. They lined up in front of Navsari Mansions like Londoners waiting for first-night seats in the pit, sine if them with stools and lunch boxes. The entire share capital was subscribed, in single shares or in blocks, by nearly nine thousand people in eight days. Later when a bond issue for 400,000 pounds was called for to provide working capital, the Maharaja Scindia of Gwalior took over the entire issue. This was a radical departure from custom, a tangible demonstration of the new spirit abroad in the land. Heretofore, Indian princes had hoarded their gold and not only balked at investing it, but would have hesitated to involve it in any project of a fellow India."*

The wealth of India had surfaced for her industrial venture.

The Initial Years

Advertisements released from the time the company started commercial production in 1912 till the end of the World War I could not be traced. The Annual Report of the company in 1907 mentions an expenditure of 18,256 rupees 15 anna and 9 paise towards advertising, printing, stamp and stationery. This was probably the expense for releasing the prospectus in the newspapers and related costs. There is no mention of advertising per se in the balance sheets of the company after 1908.

It may be noted that these were the initial years of the company. The focus was more on production and quality and the need for advertisement was limited. By October 1912 a total of 6260 tons of steel had rolled out. Steel which did not meet British Standard specifications was sent back for re melting! This was the company's first effort towards quality steel. Sales were recorded to 'Japan, China, Java, Ceylon, Burma, Straits Settlements, Australia, River Plate and the west coast of the United States. This was also the period when the modern township was being built which would later be called Jamshedpur.

The company's steel production was critical to the war supplies and well met the demands placed on it. In 1919 the Viceroy, Lord Chelmsford visited Jamshedpur appreciated the contribution by the company towards the war effort "...I can hardly imagine what we would have done if the Tata company had not given us steel for Mesopotamia, Egypt, Palestine and East Africa". He took the opportunity to officially announce the new names of Sakchi and Kalimati Railway station as Jamshedpur and Tatanagar.

The post war period, placed the Iron and Steel industry into a downward trend worldwide. This was the period the company sought to expand. Between 1924 and 1931 there was a substantial decrease in the debt capital, but the company managed to double its capacity primarily by drawing upon its depreciation reserves. This was to the discomfort of many of the share holders but almost certainly to the benefit of the Indian economy.

In the year 1925 when the management faced share holders' unrest because of its refusal to declare dividends, Mr. R D Tata sent out a landmark piece of communication to them which requested for personal sacrifice of the promoters. Owing to this passionate appeal the company eventually weathered the storm. The communication read as follows: *"We are like men building a wall against the sea. It would be the height of folly on our part to give away any part of the cement that is required to make the wall secure for all time. That is why we and you have to use this money….. to build up this great industry….. And we should not think of dividends until we have done that….Make no mistake about this point. We hold this money in trust for you. But you yourselves hold it in trust for the Indian Nation….."*

The post war period saw the formation of the first labour union in India which was set up after the strike of 1920. Since it was deemed as far from being representative, the union was denied recognition until 1925 when Mahatma Gandhi, Motilal Nehru and C F Andrews came to Jamshedpur and discussed the matter with the company management.

THE TATA IRON AND STEEL COMPANY, LIMITED.

Statement of Accounts as at 31st December 1907.

Dr. | | Cr.

CAPITAL AND LIABILITIES.	Rs. a. p.	Rs. a. p.	PROPERTY AND ASSETS.	Rs. a. p.	Rs. a. p.
Capital.			**Movable and Immovable Properties.**		
Application and Allotment Money on Ordinary, Preference and Deferred Shares	39,89,010 0 0		Ores, Concessions, Licenses, Plans, etc.	21,10,875 0 0	
Less, Allotment Money due from Shareholders	1,09,905 0 0*		Furniture and Survey Stores	4,875 8 5	21,15,750 8 5
	38,79,105 0 0		**Preliminary Expenses Chargeable to Construction Account.**		
Ordinary Shares issued as fully paid up	15,85,875 0 0	54,64,980 0 0	Printing, Advertising, Stamps and Stationery	18,256 15 9	
			Postages and Telegrams	3,200 15 3	
			Office Expenses	6,004 3 6	
			Directors' Fees	3,765 0 0	
Debts and Liabilities.			Bank's Commission and Discounts	2,652 9 2	
Deposit on account of Calls	23,828 4 6		Brokerage	1,04,072 1 0	1,37,951 12 8
Suspense Account	1,650 0 0	25,478 4 6	**Sundry Accounts.**		
			J. Kennedy Sahlin & Co., Construction Engineers' Instalment of Retaining Fee	30,000 0 0	
Profit and Loss.			Kalimati Works	5,774 13 0	35,774 13 0
Interest	10,187 9 6		**Debts owing to the Company.**		
Transfer fees	2,595 12 0	12,783 5 6	London Agents		20,436 13 0
			Cash and Investments.		
			Deposits with approved Banks	28,00,000 0 0	
			Cash—		
			With the National Bank of India, Limited, Account Current	2,88,473 6 10	
			With the Bank of India, Limited, Account Current	1,01,158 5 1	
			On hand	3,695 15 0	31,93,327 10 11
Total Rupees...		55,03,241 10 0	Total Rupees...		55,03,241 10 0

* This sum has been reduced to Rs. 91,810 up to the 4th Instant.

TATA SONS & Co.,
Agents.

Bombay, 7th February 1908.

The Swadeshi Theme

It was in the post war decade, that companies such as The Tinplate Company of India, Indian Wire Products and Agriculture Implements Limited were formed. The latter was acquired by Tata Steel to become Tata Agrico – in a way the company's first brand. The first advertisements that were released in 1928 maintain the Swadeshi spirit by including the catch line 'buy Indian Steel'. The 'Swadeshi' feeling was further reinforced in an advertisement of 1930 which was released in the Leader, from Allahabad which implores the Indian to buy Tata instead of foreign steel. By 1925 the company had already been termed the Pittsburgh of India and in a report in the The Indian Daily Mail in the year 1925, there was a detailed account on the formation of the company and its then production processes.

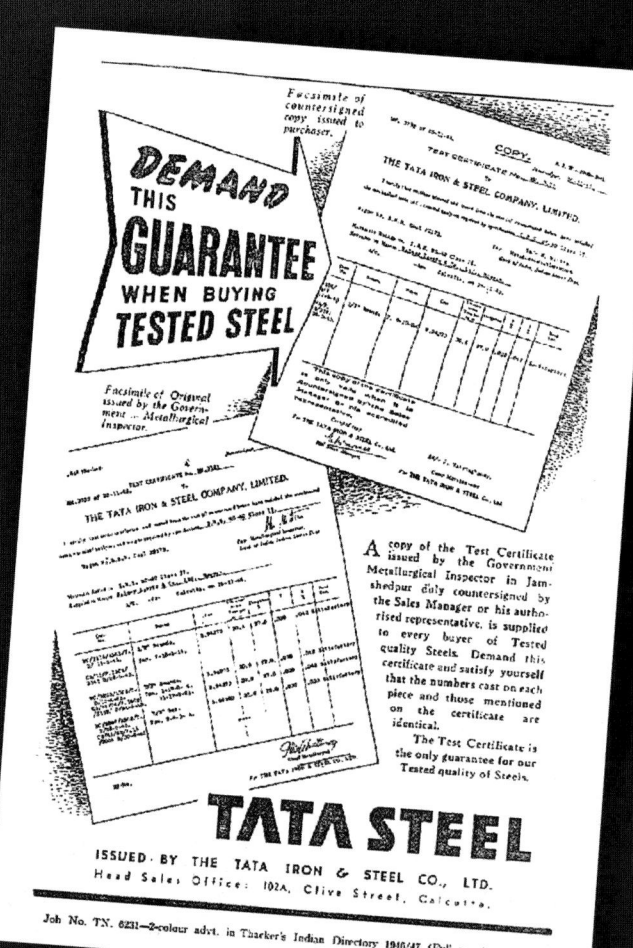

By now operations inside Asia's first and only integrated steel plant were in full swing. It was only natural that demand for its steel started coming from across the oceans. This probably inspired the line 'The Company's Steel Works are the largest and Best Equipped in the British Empire', which was incorporated in many advertisements of that period.

The copy also focused on the product mix and educated the reader on the quality of steel being produced conforming to British Standard Specifications. In fact the advertisements requested the customers to insist on a test certificate which was in accordance to the laid specifications, setting the foundation for a brand people would trust the world over.

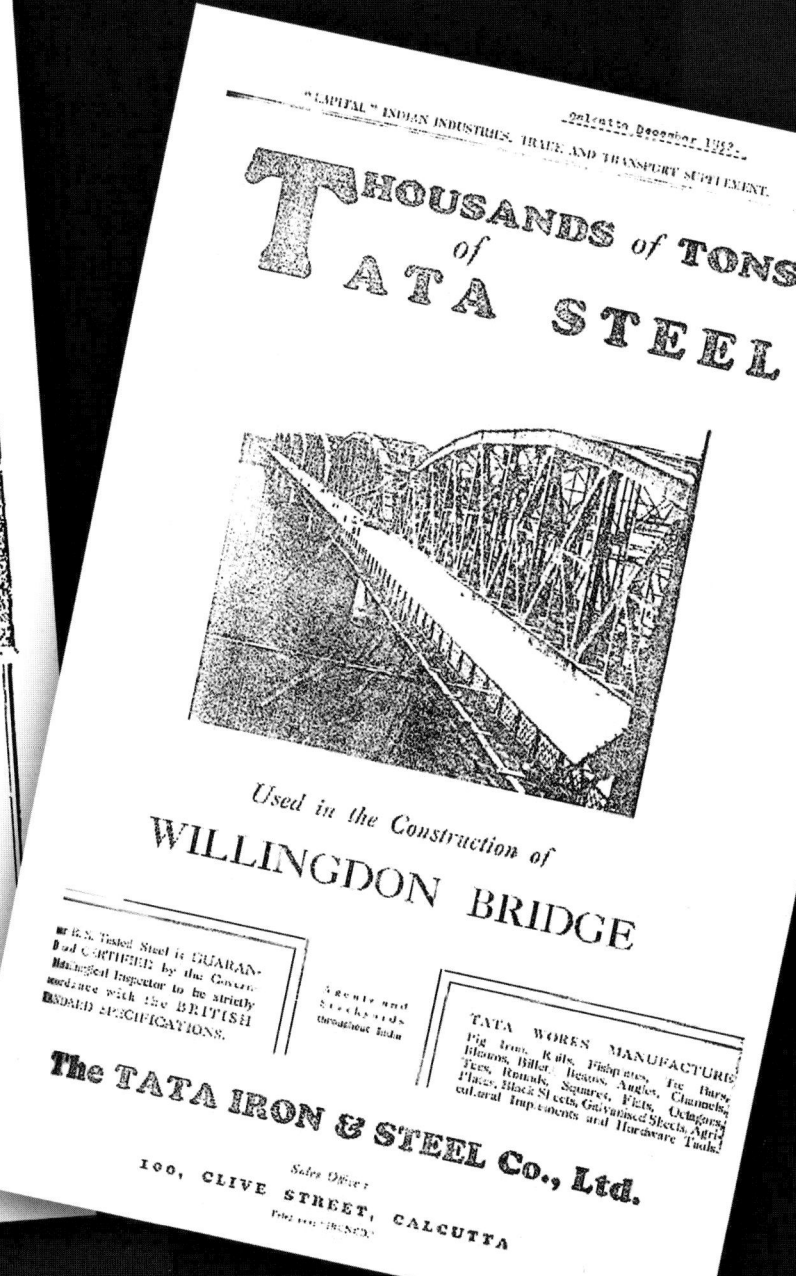

The company released these (first?) testimonial based advertisements in the Calcutta Municipal Gazette and the supplement of the Capital Indian Industries. The advertisements spoke of the supply of steel in the making of the Bally Bridge in Kolkata and the Willingdon Bridge in South India.

[SEPTEMBER 22, 1923.] THE CHAMBER OF COMMERCE JOURNAL.

JAMSHEDPUR
INDIA.

Commemorating the name of Jamsetji Tata, founder of

THE TATA IRON & STEEL Co. Ltd.

whose works, subsidiaries, town, dairy and sewage farms cover an area of 8 square miles, which 20 years ago was jungle.

36" 3-High Plate Mill.

PRESENT PRODUCTION CAPACITY — { 600,000 tons Pig Iron, 500,000 tons Steel Ingots. }

PRODUCTS: Rails and Fishplates, Sections, Boiler and Ship Plates (all to British Standard Specification), Tin Bar, Sheet Bar, Sleeper Plates, Pressed Steel Sleepers, Black and Galvanised Sheets, Agricultural Implements, Ferro Manganese, Sulphuric Acid, Sulphate of Ammonia, Coal Tar.

Head Office: **TATA SONS LTD., 24, Bruce Street, Fort, BOMBAY.**

JAMSHEDPUR WORKS:
Tatanagar Station, B.N. Rly. (150 Miles West of Calcutta).

LONDON AGENTS:
Tata Ltd.
Capel House, New Broad Street, London, E.C.2.

Cutting from the "Indian Finance".
Calcutta, Saturday, December 17 1932.

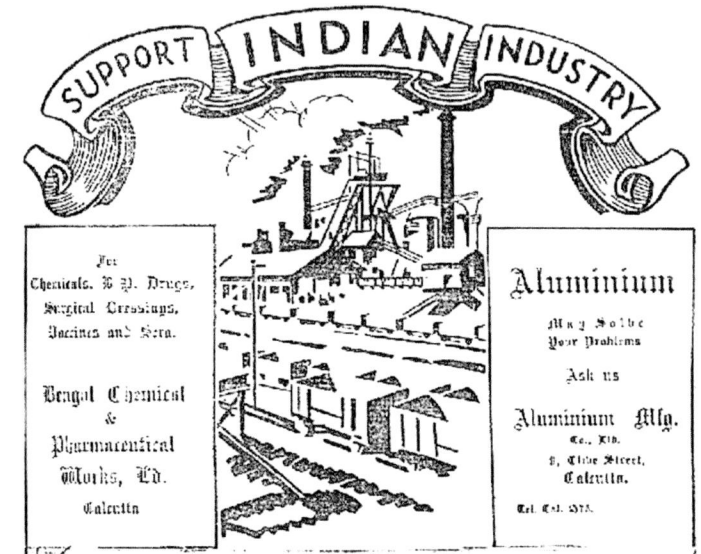

TATA STEEL

Is Manufactured up to any standard specification in India by Indian Labour.

All our B.S. tested steel is GUARANTEED and CERTIFIED by the Government Metallurgical Inspector to be strictly in accordance with the BRITISH STANDARD SPECIFICATIONS. INSIST ON having our Test Certificate when ordering B.S. Tested Steel.

TATA WORKS
MANUFACTURE:

Pig Iron, Blooms, Billets, Rails, Fishplates, Tie Bars, Sleepers, Joists, Angles, Channels, Tees, Rounds, Squares, Flats, Octagons, Plates, Black Sheets, Galvanised Plain and Corrugated Sheets, Agricultural Implements and Hardware Tools.

Agents & Stockyards Throughout India:

THE TATA IRON & STEEL CO., LTD.

Sales Office: 100, Clive Street, CALCUTTA.
Telegrams: "IRONCO".

THE LEADER, THURSDAY, OCTOBER 9,

WHY FOREIGN STEEL

WHEN

TATA IS CHEAPER

BUY YOUR OWN NATIONAL STEEL BECAUSE TATA STEEL MEANS INDIAN CAPITAL AND INDIAN LABOUR
USE TATA STEEL AND YOU HELP INDIA

TATA WORKS MANUFACTURE

Billets, Beams, Angles Channels, Tees, Rounds, Squares, Flats, Octagons, Plates, Black Sheets, Galv: Sheets, Agricultural Implements and Hardware Tools

AGENTS THROUGHOUT INDIA

DEPOTS:—Ambala, Bareilly, Benares, Dehradun, Dharampur (Simla Hills), Gujranwala, Lucknow, Meerut, Mirzapur, Ranchi, Rangoon, Rawalpindi, Saharanpur and Sungrur

STOCK-YARDS:—Bombay, Calcutta (Shalimar), Cawnpur, Sihala (Near Rawalpindi), Jallo, Near Lahore), Jallundur, Madras, Meerut and Nagpur.

THE TATA IRON & STEEL CO., LTD.

Sales Office:
100, CLIVE STREET CALCUTTA
Works & General Manager's Office.
JAMSHEDPUR, via TATANAGAR, B. N. R.
Managing Agents

MESSRS TATA SONS LIMITED

"Bombay House," 24, Bruce Street, Fort Bombay.

THE TATA IRON & STEEL COMPANY, LIMITED.

Facts that speak for themselves.

72% of India's requirements of steel in 1932-33 were supplied by the Company.

The Company employs over **20,000 people** hailing from all parts of India.

SIXTEEN trains steam into the Company's Works daily bringing in raw materials for the manufacture of Iron & Steel.

ELEVEN trains steam out of Jamshedpur daily to distribute the manufactured products of the Steel Works to all parts of India.

Nearly **ONE-THIRD OF** the total public traffic of the Bengal Nagpur Railway is provided by THE COMPANY.

BUY INDIAN STEEL.
SUPPORT INDIAN INDUSTRY.

The company released several advertisements in trade journals and magazines thereby catering to a niche audience, as is evident of its releases in The Indian Finance, The Financial News and The Chamber of Commerce Journal. The copy delved on the 'menu' of products, the standard based specifications and the expanding network of the company. The advertisement in the Financial News gave facts on rail movement to and from the Works, employment generation and the fact that the company had supplied 72% of the Nation's steel requirements. The advertisements showed maturity in communicating various facets of the steel business and its potential.

તાતા સ્ટીલ

હીંદી રેલ્વે સ્ટેન્ડર્ડ અને બ્રીટીશ સ્ટેન્ડર્ડનાં
સ્પેશીફીકેશનો મુજબનું હીંદમાં બનાવેલું

તમારી જરૂરીયાતો માટે નીચેનું મેળવવાની હઠ લ્યો.

તાતા ખીમ્સ	તાતા ચેનલ્સ	તાતા રેલ્સ
તાતા આર્સ	તાતા ઍંગલ્સ	તાતા ફીશપ્લેટસ
તાતા શીટસ	તાતા શઉડસ	તાતા સ્લીપર્સ
તાતા પ્લેટસ	તાતા ટીઝ	તાતા સ્કવેર્સ

અને તાતા હાઇ ટેનસાઇલ સ્ટીલ

ધી તાતા આર્યન એન્ડ સ્ટીલ કંપની લીમીટેડ.

સેલ્સ ઓફીસ–૧૦૦ કલાઇવ સ્ટ્રીટ, કલકતા.
શાખા ઓફીસ–૨૪ બરુસ સ્ટ્રીટ, ફોર્ટ, મુંબઇ.

The company had by this period recognised the need to address its audience in the regional languages. Keeping the 'swadeshi' theme alive it released advertisements for Tata Agrico in Gujarati. This was probably the first advertisement in a regional language by the company.

તા. ૨૧ મી ઓકટોબર ૧૯૩૦

દીપોત્સવી અંક

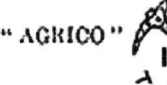 "AGRICO" 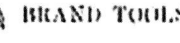 BRAND TOOLS

સ્વદેશી ખનીજ પદાર્થ, સ્વદેશી થાપણુ, અને મુખ્યત્વે દેશી કામદારોને હાથે બનતી લોખંડ અને પોલાદની પેદાયશો.

ધી તાતા આયર્ન
એન્ડ
સ્ટીલ કંપની, લી૦

તમોને લોખંડ અને પોલાદની લગભગ સઘળી જરૂરીઆતો પુરી પાડશે. અને તેમાં બાંધકામને માટે જોઇતી ચીજો,—બીમ્સ, એંગલ્સ, ચેનલ્સ, બાર્સ, વીગેરે—તે ઉપરાંત ખાસ તમામ

 **હાર્ડવેર**

ને નામે ઓળખાતી ચીજો જેવી કે

જાતજાતના પાવડા, ત્રીકમ, નરાજ, કુહાડીઓ, હથોડા, છીણી, કોદાળી રેલ્વે બીટર્સ વિગેરે સઘળી ક્યાંઇ પણ દેશમાં બનતી એ કીસમની પેદાશો સાથે હરીફાઇ અને સરસાઇ કરે એવી ઉંચી જાતની પુરી પાડી શકે છે. અને તદ્દન કીફાયત ભાવે પુરી પાડશે.

એ વિષે કું૦ ની મુંબઇની હેડ ઓફીસ, અગર કું૦ ના જમશેદપુરનાં કારખાના ઉપર લખો.

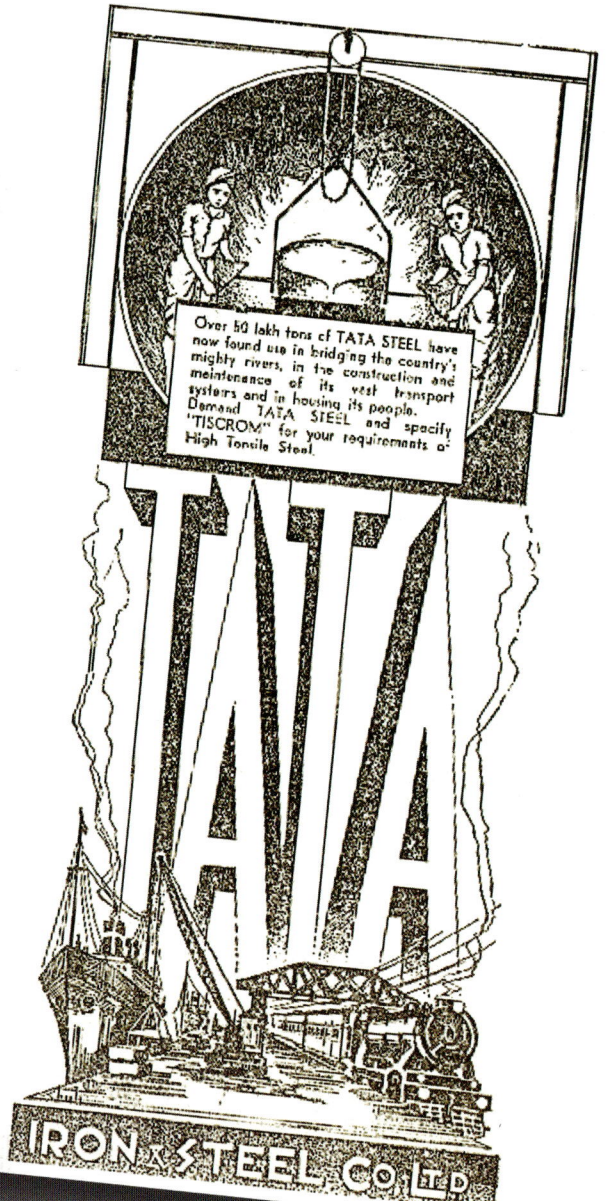

The advertisements till date had always carried the company name in full - The Tata Iron and Steel Company Limited. However the word Tata was used in different forms and fonts to emphasise the name of Tata. One advertisement for structural steel, carried a mnemonic showing an Indian warrior holding a steel sword and the words Steel Strength. This, however, was never used again.

THE TIMES OF INDIA, 23-5-34

THE TATA IRON AND STEEL CO., LTD.,
BOMBAY HOUSE, 24, BRUCE STREET,
FORT, BOMBAY.

(ENGINEERING SUPPLEMENT)

ADVERTISEMENT

a mighty dam

or the delicate hairspring of a watch

IN building a giant dam—harnessing the Nation's power resources — or making the delicate mechanism of a watch—Steel is indispensable. The world processes of modern production and distribution in their impressive vastness and endless ramifications depend, in one way or another, on Steel.

We are the pioneers in rolled Steel Production in India from indigenous basic raw materials. Our Steel Works is the largest and most modern of its kind in the East.

Nearly a quarter of a century of Steel-making experience and absolute control of raw materials and processes, from mines to mills, are your guarantee of quality and dependability in purchasing Tata Steel.

BUY TATA STEEL AND NO OTHER.

The Tata Iron & Steel Co., Ltd.

Sales Office : 100, Clive Street, CALCUTTA.

BRANCH SALES OFFICES:—

BOMBAY	Bombay House, 24, Bruce Street, Fort.
MADRAS	108, Armenian Street.
LAHORE	The Mall.
CAWNPORE	Cooperganj.
HATHRAS	Hathras Jn., E. I. Ry.
PATNA	Exhibition Road.
SECUNDERABAD	52, Sebastian Road, (Deccan).
NAGPUR	Itwari Bazar.
VIZIANAGRAM	Vizianagram Cantonment.
SABARMATI	Sabarmati Oil Mills Compound.

Till 1935 steel had remained a faceless commodity in India. This changed in 1935 when the company announced TISCROM - a high tensile steel. This was the first branded product from Tata Steel. The advertisement was subsequently released in several regional languages.

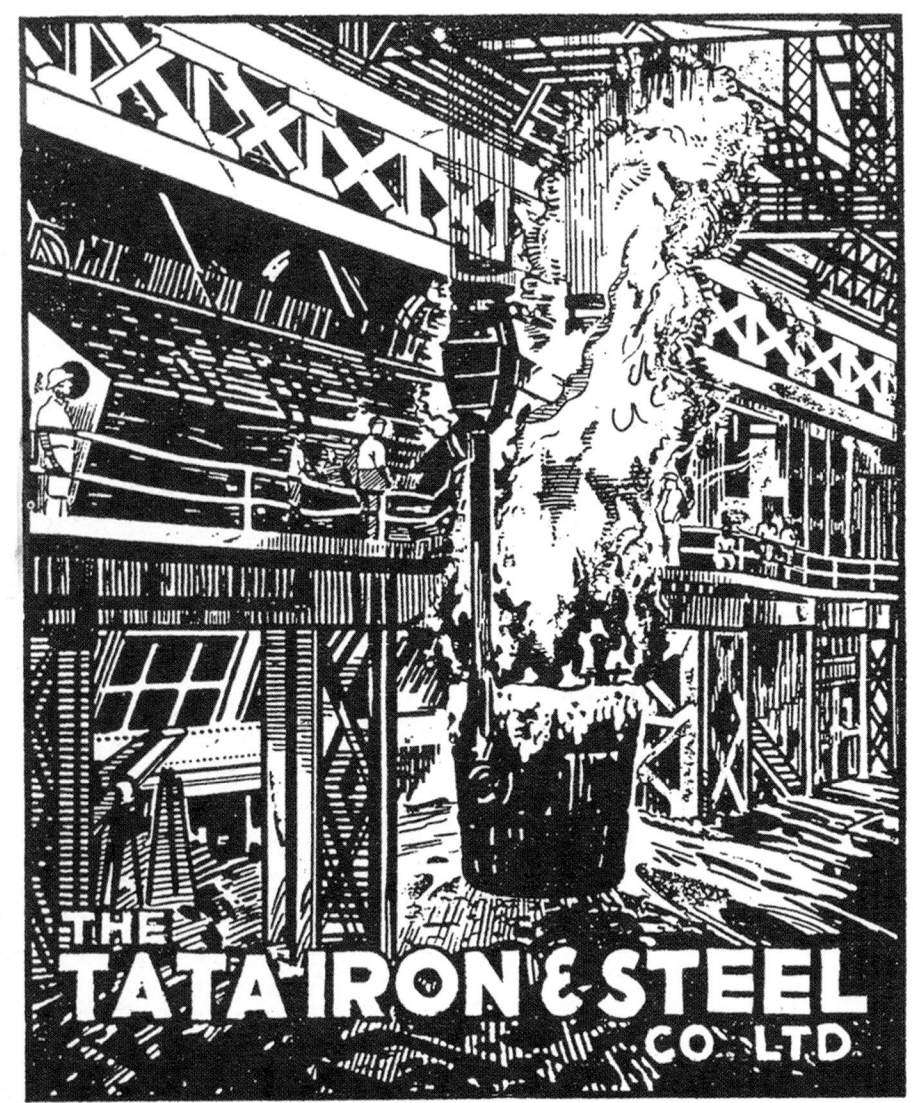

By 1934 the company was supplying steel for almost all major infrastructure and manufacturing industries. A corporate advertisement released in the 1934 annual of the Times of India spoke about the product range and the network reach. This was one of the first of the several corporate campaigns. It was also perhaps the first colour advertisement.

Text from the Times of India Annual 1934

India's Iron & Steel

The production of pig iron on a commercial basis in India dates back to the year 1875, when the Bengal Iron and Steel Company established a factory at Kulti. In the earlier stages of its existence this company experienced many difficulties, the extent of which may be judged by the fact that it made practically no profits for thirty years….

But whereas the Bengal Iron Company started in a small way and built up its business gradually, the Tata Iron and Steel company at Jamshedpur spent 5 years in construction works and commenced active production in the year 1912 as a ready-made concern. It is true that many extensions have since been added; and it is equally true that business conditions and business methods were radically different in 1875 to when they were in 1912, but the difference in policy remain.

To begin with the management of the Tata Iron and Steel Company deliberately sought a tract of land devoid of villages, having a potentially suitable water supply, and within reasonable distance of a trunk railway which again would give easy connection with the available sources of iron ore; and they found such a spot on the northern side of the Bengal-Nagpur Railway some two hundred miles west of Calcutta. And here, in what was practically virgin jungle, they set out to construct a modern iron and steel works and to erect a complete township for the housing of the huge number of workmen who would have to be employed.

TATA GALVANIZED STEEL SHEETS

THE ALL PURPOSES MATERIAL

TATA

That India is becoming more and more galvanized sheet conscious is evidenced from the increasing popularity of Tata products in this field.

Indian consumers are rapidly realizing the tremendous possibilities of this all-purposes material which costs so little to buy, less still to erect, and nothing whatever to maintain. Plain galvanized sheets are available for tank-building, bucket-making and a wide variety of uses. Corrugated galvanized sheets, in which the inherently great strength of steel is multiplied tenfold by scientific shaping, do sterling duty in village and city, cottage and factory.

Tata's experts are always pleased to give advice on problems connected with galvanized steel sheets.

ISSUED BY THE TATA IRON & STEEL COMPANY, LIMITED.

TN·104

With the Great Expansion Programme of the 1920s a new sheet mill was set up with galvanising facilities. This mill produced plain as well as corrugated sheets. Till the mid 30s the product - Galvanised Plain and Corrugated Sheets — were mentioned in the advertisements but no dedicated campaign was released until after the TISCROM brand was announced. The product was in great demand as its versatile usage served well in a country with varied geographies and topography. It was obvious that GC Sheets would also be sold under a brand name and the brand 'Tata Sun' was born.

In its early campaigns the product was introduced as 'an all purpose material' and later in a four part campaign, the theme 'Nation's Choice' was introduced.

The product was extensively supplied to the Allied forces in the erection of the Anderson Bomb Shelters. A news report in The Statesman in the year 1940, which talked about the strength of the Anderson shelter, was used effectively as a testimonial advertisement.

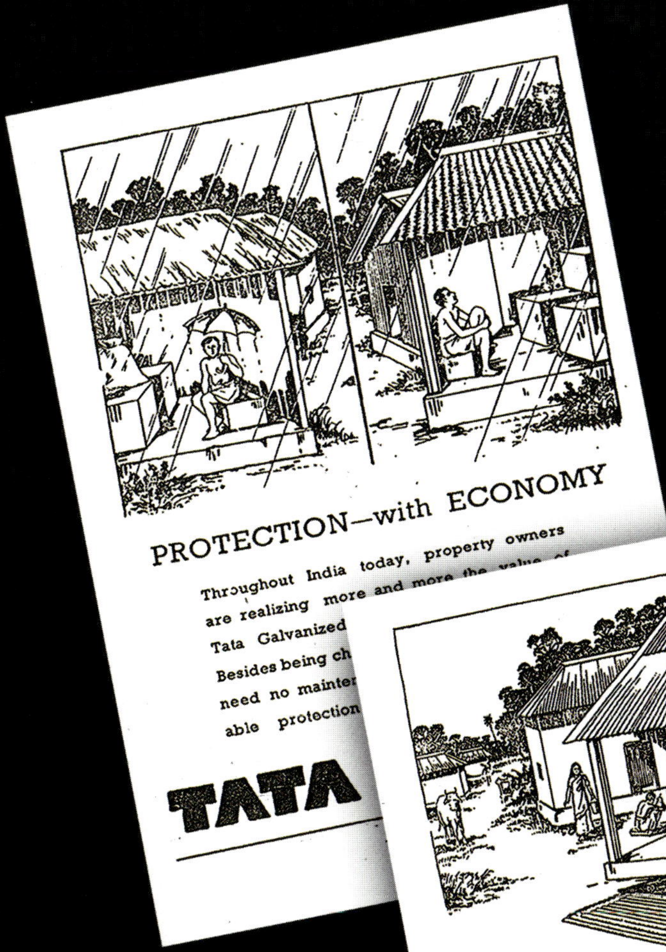
PROTECTION—with ECONOMY
Throughout India today, property owners
are realizing more and more the value of
Tata Galvanized
Besides being ch
need no mainte
able protection
TATA

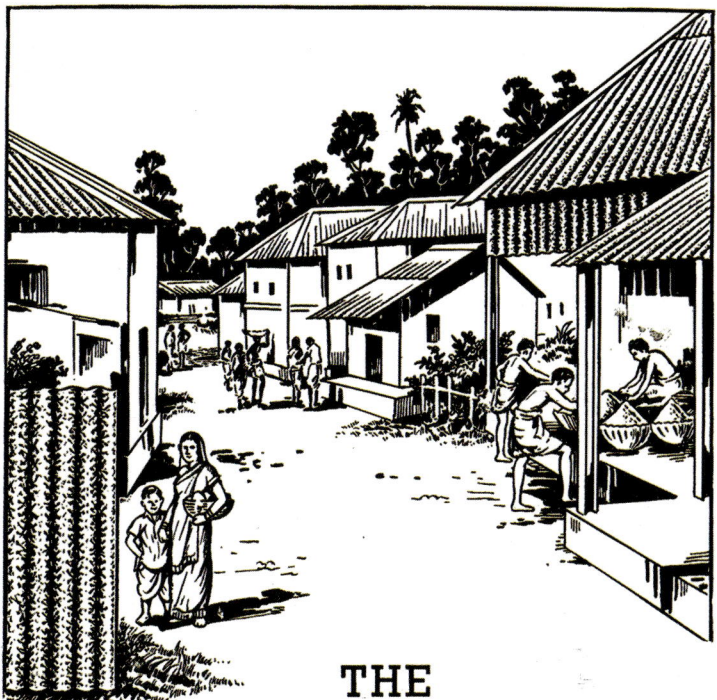

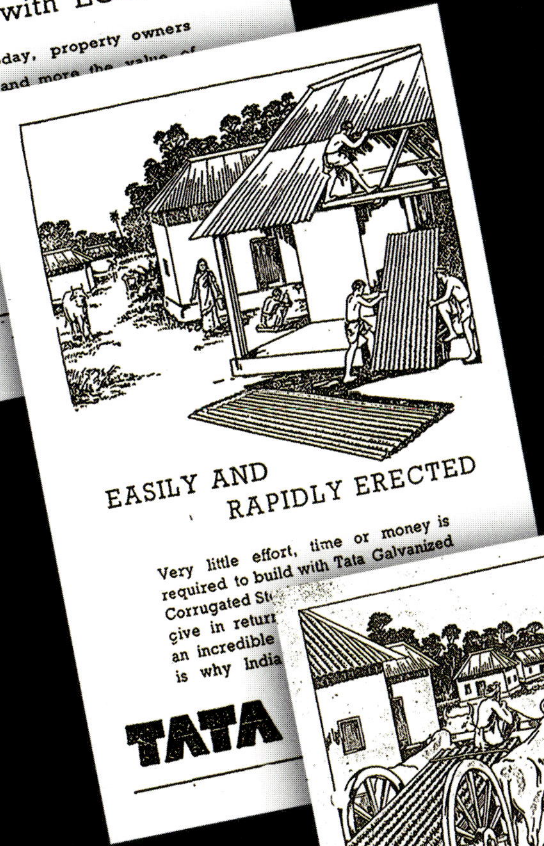
EASILY AND
RAPIDLY ERECTED
Very little effort, time or money is
required to build with Tata Galvanized
Corrugated St
give in retur
an incredible
is why India
TATA

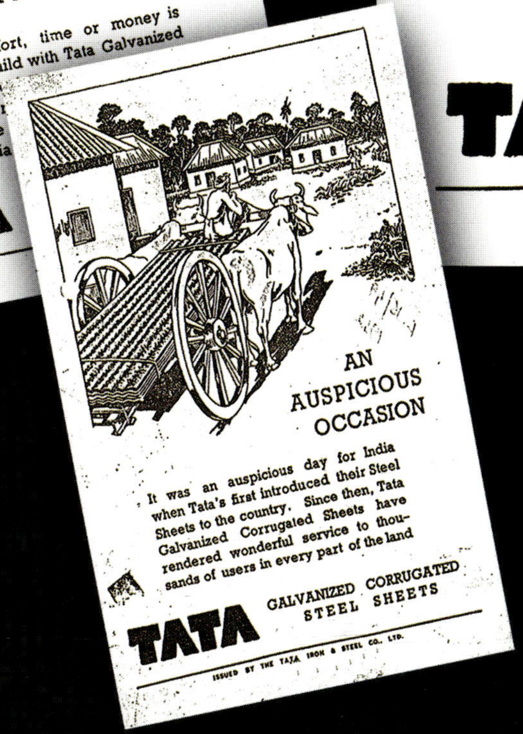
AN
AUSPICIOUS
OCCASION
It was an auspicious day for India
when Tata's first introduced their Steel
Sheets to the country. Since then, Tata
Galvanized Corrugated Sheets have
rendered wonderful service to thou-
sands of users in every part of the land
TATA
GALVANIZED CORRUGATED
STEEL SHEETS
ISSUED BY THE TATA IRON & STEEL CO., LTD.

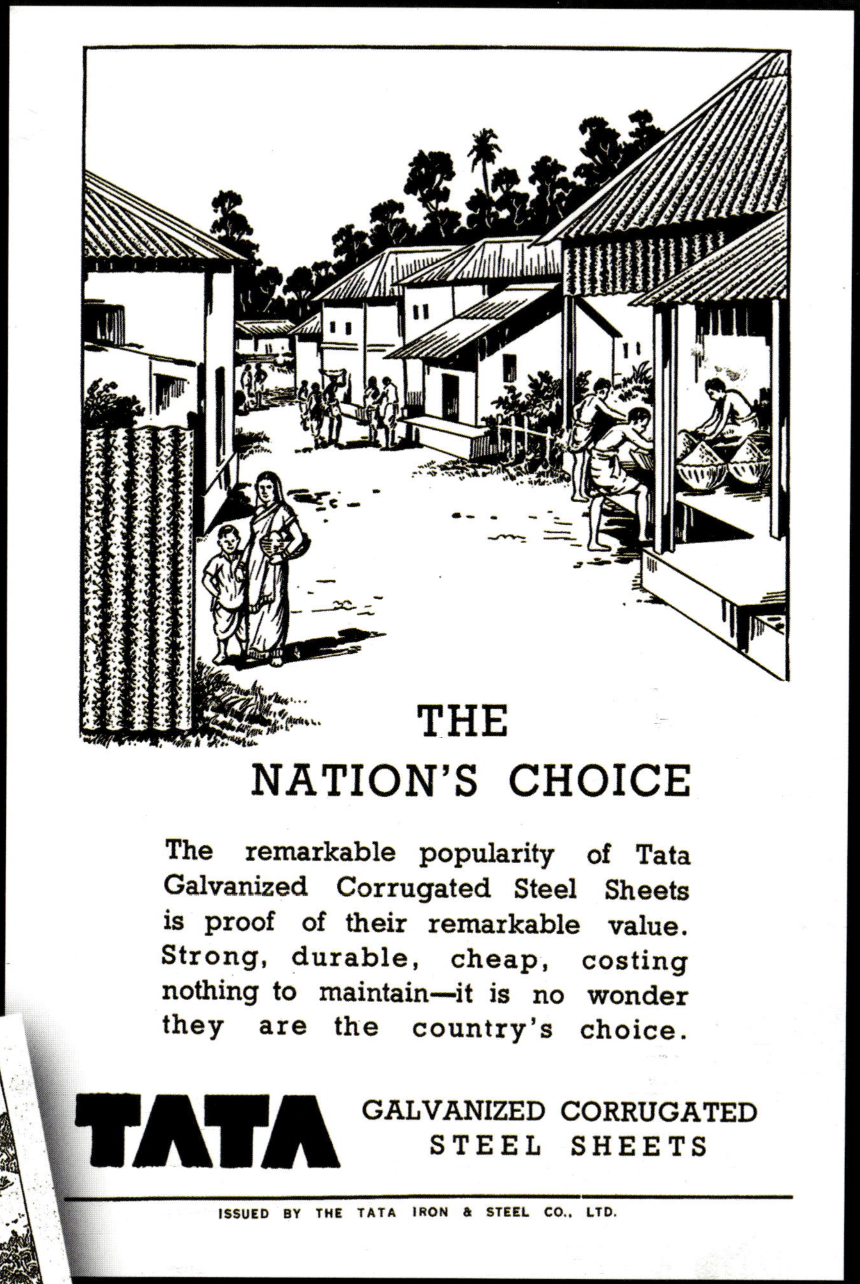
THE
NATION'S CHOICE
The remarkable popularity of Tata
Galvanized Corrugated Steel Sheets
is proof of their remarkable value.
Strong, durable, cheap, costing
nothing to maintain—it is no wonder
they are the country's choice.
TATA
GALVANIZED CORRUGATED
STEEL SHEETS
ISSUED BY THE TATA IRON & STEEL CO., LTD.

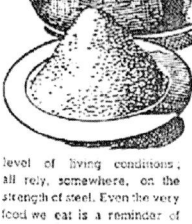
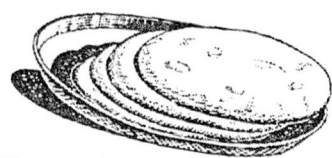

In its campaign 'Steel and …' the copy reinforced the fact that steel machinery, components and articles aided in the production of foodstuffs and textiles too. The advertisements signed off with the line 'Steel is of greatest economic importance to the life of the country.'

This campaign was a real milestone in annals of the Indian Advertising industry promoting the use of the product rather than the company itself.

SCOB

The Indian Iron and Steel Company (IISCO) founded by British interests in Calcutta, primarily for the production of pig iron, acquired the defunct 'Bengal Iron Company'. In 1936 The Steel Corporation of Bengal (SCOB) was formed by the IISCO management.

Tata Steel's association with SCOB was a unique initiative. It was one of the first marketing tie-ups that the company had with an outside entity. In the company's Annual Report of 1938-39 it is mentioned that "...a preliminary working arrangement has been entered into with the Steel Corporation of Bengal Ltd., in regard to the sale of certain common products of the two companies. This agreement which will come into force when the Bengal Corporation are able to put their products on the market will, it is hope, work to the benefit of both parties by minimizing distribution costs and avoiding uneconomic competition."

Subsequently, in the Annual Report of the following year it is mentioned that "...a central sales office has been established in the Steel Company's sales office in Calcutta for dealing with bars, structurals and rails which may be jointly produced by the company and the Steel Corporation of Bengal. It is hoped that this co-operation between these two steel producing companies will tend to promote the general interest of the steel industry in India."

The marketing arrangement saw a series of joint advertisement campaigns that drove home the point that steel was a very versatile product with huge potential.

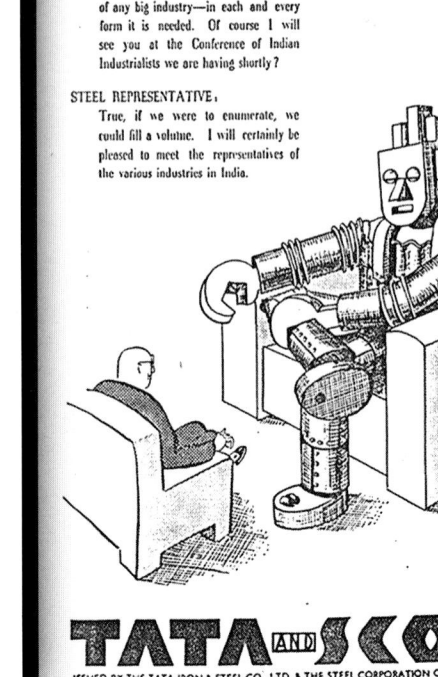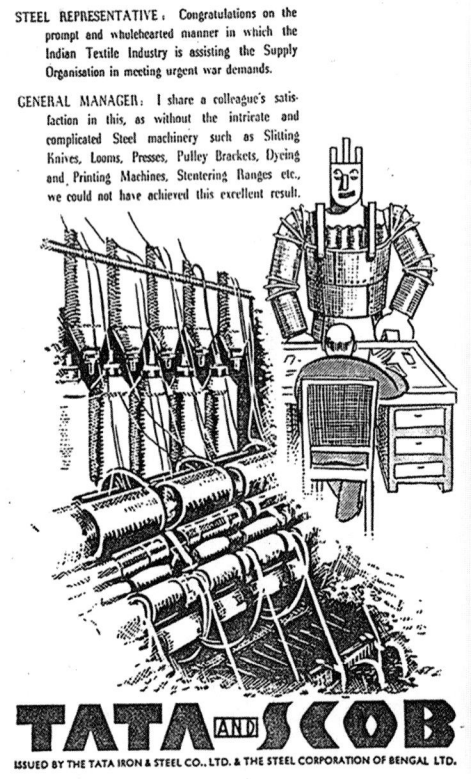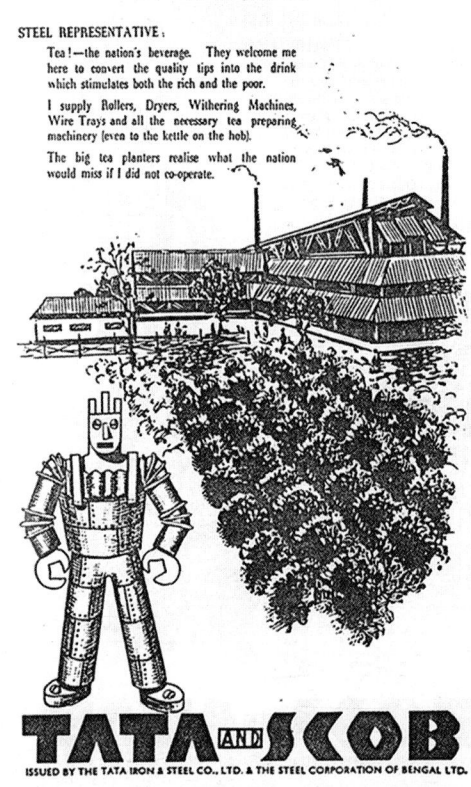

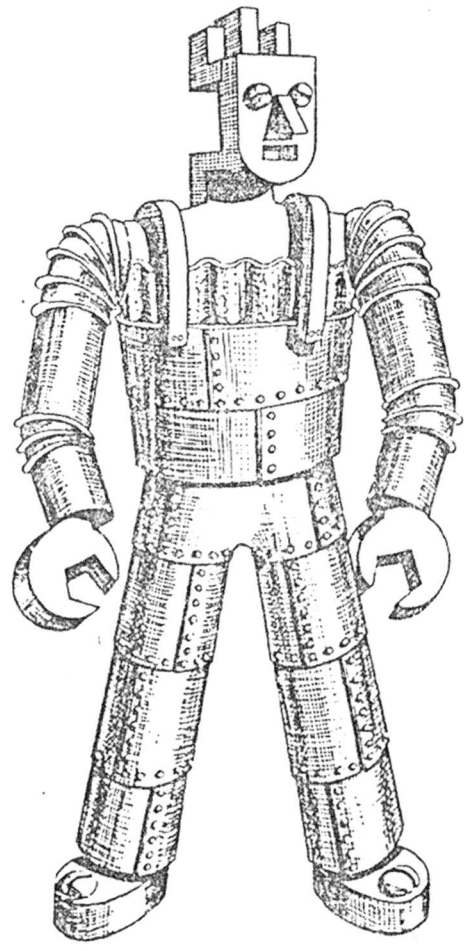

The Steel Representative

In 1942, a unique campaign was launched by the company and SCOB - where a figure of a man made of steel was shown representing the steel industry. This Steel Representative talks to farmers, people in the Works, jute workers, production managers, etc. over a series of twelve advertisements. This was perhaps for the first time in the Indian advertising industry that a mnemonic was effectively used to communicate the importance of steel in the different facets of industry.

Many campaigns were released during the arrangement with SCOB. The advertisements were designed to project the marvel of steel and its varied usage in transportation and everyday life.

The advertisements commenced in 1936/37 and continued till after the end of the Great War. It is evident from the SCOB and the other advertisements that the company had retained the advertising agency J Walter Thompson to design and release the advertisements. This agency had opened its office (1930?) in India to look after the General Motors account (the agency still continues to be with Tata Steel).

From Indian Mythology..

The Hindu mythology, Ramayana and Bhagavata, tells us that Indra, the King of Devas, flew across the skies in his chariot, by virtue of his supernatural powers — beyond human comprehension.

To-day, we see the modern flying chariot — the Aeroplane — amazing in speed and efficiency. Pause  to reflect for a moment and you will realise that the Aeroplane would be impossible without STEEL

TATA and SCOB

STEEL BRINGS PROSPERITY

ISSUED BY THE TATA IRON & STEEL CO. LTD. & THE STEEL CORPORATION OF BENGAL LTD.

Time and Tide...

Vagaries of nature are no longer serious obstacles to international commerce. Science and progress have surmounted the dangers of ocean transport. Gigantic modern liners plough the seas at all hours of the day and night speedily carrying goods and passengers in safety and comfort.

STEEL has contributed in no small measure to this progress. A glance at a modern ship from stem to stern will at once indicate that from the humble screw and rivet to the gigantic boilers and engines, STEEL has been used in a variety of ways for the construction of the liner.

TATA and SCOB

STEEL BRINGS PROSPERITY

ISSUED BY THE TATA IRON & STEEL CO., LTD. & THE STEEL CORPORATION OF BENGAL LTD.

SERENADE TO STEEL

Music has always been a source of delight and inspiration.

Through steel gramophone needles and sound-box we can hear the music we love best whenever we wish.

Into a busy world, steel brings joy and relaxation.

TATA and SCOB

Issued by
The Tata Iron & Steel Co., Ltd. & The Steel Corporation of Bengal Ltd.

MIGHTIER THAN THE SWORD...

Steel nibs have altered history and constantly control our lives.

In every phase of life steel is an essential, vital factor.

TATA and SCOB

Issued by
The Tata Iron & Steel Co., Ltd. & The Steel Corporation of Bengal Ltd.

A campaign that reinforced the fact that 'in every phase of life, steel is an essential, vital factor'.

Making Dreams Come True

Modest bolts and nuts of steel, translate ambitious blue prints into imposing edifices.

Discreetly imbedded at vital points, these steel pigmies create giants of industry.

ALWAYS—EVERYWHERE—STEEL FOR STRENGTH

ISSUED BY THE TATA IRON & STEEL CO., LTD. HEAD SALES OFFICE : 102A, CLIVE STREET, CALCUTTA.

Building Tomorrow's India

To prepare for tomorrow the myriad tools of Industry beat and clang today.

It is on the spanner, the screwdriver, the wrench, the hammer—that Industrial Progress depends.

In every tool and instrument rendering service in the cause of Progress—it is the strength of steel which gives them the dependability they *must* possess.

ALWAYS—EVERYWHERE—STEEL FOR STRENGTH

ISSUED BY THE TATA IRON & STEEL CO., LTD. HEAD SALES OFFICE : 102A, CLIVE STREET, CALCUTTA.

Mighty Atom...

Only a cog—yet equally important in delicate mechanisms and giant machinery. The progress of industry depends upon such vital parts as these. For strength and reliability we turn to steel, of which these vital parts are made.

ALWAYS—EVERYWHERE—STEEL FOR STRENGTH

ISSUED BY THE TATA IRON & STEEL CO., LTD. HEAD SALES OFFICE : 102A, CLIVE STREET, CALCUTTA.

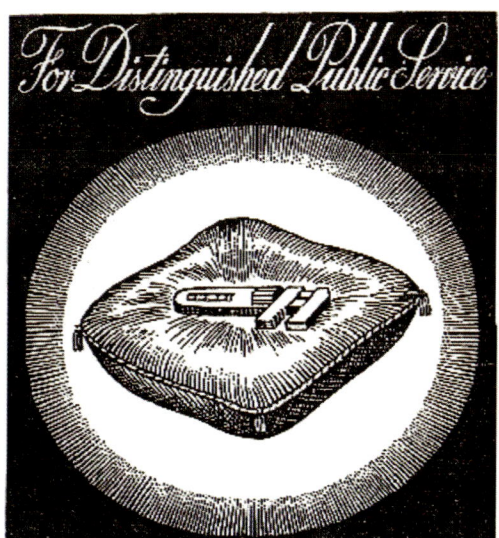

The appointment of a professional agency led to a clarity in theme and thought. Of the many campaigns that were designed and released by the agency there was one that had the caption 'Always-Everywhere-Steel for strength'. This campaign visually captured the use of steel in various tools of trade.

Another advertisement designed with this theme showed a dressing table and spoke about the 'part' that steel played in making all the products displayed on the table.

In 1941 Tata Steel introduced the concept of greeting stakeholders and the nation by releasing advertisements on festival days. This practice continued for years. These days festival greetings are commonly used by brands to wish their target audience.

World War II

There was a great demand for steel from the company to cater to the needs of the Second Great War. This was also the period of an Extension Programme within the Steel works. A Wheel, an Axle and a Tyre plant was planned along with a billet mill and a strip mill.

The war effort by the company did not limit itself to the production of special steel for defence and communication purposes. In the company's Annual Report of 1940/41 a detailed account on the company's contribution to the war effort in terms of production, training and logistics is mentioned.

'During the year under review the Company co-operated with Government to its utmost capacity in the furtherance of the war effort. In spite of the very heavy demands on its staff, 74 employees have been permitted to take up special work in connection with the war and have already joined duty. These include seven employees from Jamshedpur who have been selected under the Bevin Scheme and have left for special training in England.

At the request of the Government, the Company has undertaken to train mechanics for the Indian Air Force Reserve and war technicians for the Army Ordnance Corps. On the 31st March 1941, there were 100 Air Force mechanics and 45 war technicians on the rolls of the Institute at Jamshedpur.

The manufacture of bullet proof armour plate steel has been successfully developed and such steel is being made for the requirements of armoured vehicles in India. Special steels have also been developed for armour piercing bullets and shells, for machine guns as well as for rifle and machine gun magazines and for drawing into telegraph wires.

Research has been successfully pursued in connection wit the welding of chrome molybdenum steel required for aircraft.

The advice and assistance of the Company's experts has been fully placed at the disposal of Government in connection with their own problems in the manufacture of special steels. As a result of its activities, particularly since the war, the Company is now in a position to manufacture a large variety of special steels which had so far been imported'.

The citizens of Jamshedpur contributed in their special way and gifted the Royal Air Force a Spitfire aircraft that was aptly christened 'The spirit of Golmuri' by the RAF.

In the advertisements released during the war years, the copy delved upon the need of the hour and as to how the company was catering to the currents demands. At the same time the copy was also worded to speak about how steel would be used in normal life when 'peace returns'.

GUNS BEFORE GRAMOPHONES

The manufacture of the intricate and delicate machinery of a modern gramophone demands special alloy and stainless steel for accuracy and endurance.

In the present conflict, human lives may depend upon the reliability of such special steels, which we supply for the equally intricate construction of gun carriers and tanks.

When peace returns to the world our special steels will be available for the manufacture of tools, machinery, gramophones and for the manifold requirements of normal life.

TATA
SPECIAL ALLOY & TOOL
STEELS

ISSUED BY THE TATA IRON & STEEL CO., LTD.
HEAD SALES OFFICE: 102A, CLIVE STREET, CALCUTTA.

BALING OUT ON A TYPEWRITER

The metal in the harness of a parachute is made of special high tensile and alloy steels to ensure the safety of the life it carries.

In times of peace such steels are used in the manufacture of dies for typewriters and for many other essentials and luxuries of everyday life.

Today military requirements have first claim on all the special steel we manufacture. The growth of India's post-war Industry is our next concern.

TATA
SPECIAL ALLOY & TOOL
STEELS

ISSUED BY THE TATA IRON & STEEL CO., LTD.
HEAD SALES OFFICE: 102A, CLIVE STREET, CALCUTTA.

SPECIAL ALLOY & TOOL STEEL

The manufacture of cloth, soap, perfumes and other products of our day to day life is facilitated by the use of special Steel equipment. In many other fields where strength and resistance to heat or corrosion are required special steels are specified.

Until recently India has been dependent entirely on imports for these indispensable tools in her struggle for industrialisation. Now confident of the expansion of Indian Industries in the post-war world, the works at Jamshedpur have been equipped to meet such future demands.

At the moment, military requirements have prior claim on all the special steels we manufacture; the experience we are gaining now coupled with the results of the continued research carried out in our laboratories will be available to meet the demands on us when peace returns.

TATA
SPECIAL ALLOY & TOOL
STEELS

Issued by the Tata Iron & Steel Co., Ltd.
Head Sales Office: 102-A, Clive Street, Calcutta.

BOMBS BEFORE BICYCLES

The manufacture of bicycles requires a number of special alloy and tool steels to produce a reliable article.

Just now we are supplying these steels to case the bombs our aircraft carry far into enemy territory, and for other demands of war production.

When bombs become obsolete, we will be ready with our special steels for peace-time industry for dies, machine tools, bicycles and many other requirements of modern production.

TATA
SPECIAL ALLOY & TOOL
STEELS

ISSUED BY THE TATA IRON & STEEL CO., LTD.
HEAD SALES OFFICE: 102A, CLIVE STREET, CALCUTTA.

With the development of the special alloy and tool steels the company released a campaign which had the signature line 'Tata Special Alloy & Tool Steels'

India will keep on delivering the goods...

...WITH BARGES MADE FROM TATA STEEL

In the effort for victory, the steady stream of supplies from India plays a part of ever increasing importance. A vital link in this scheme is the humble barge. Along the waterways of India these silent vessels come, carrying their precious cargoes—the very sinews of war. It is on the strength of steel, from which these barges are made, that the men who need those supplies have learnt to depend.

 **STEEL FOR STRENGTH**

ISSUED BY THE TATA IRON & STEEL CO., LTD. HEAD SALES OFFICE: 102A, CLIVE St., CALCUTTA

"INDIAN CRAFTSMEN CAN BE PROUD OF TATANAGARS" *Says Army Observer with the 8th Army*

"Safer than slit-trenches during a bombing raid," was a Gunner officer's tribute to the 'Tatanagars'—the armoured cars made in India which have been doing remarkable service in the Eighth Army's forward drive.

The officer went on to describe how, while he was moving his Observation Post forward, a 75 m.m. shell burst on one side of his 'Tatanagar.' The metal plates were buckled, but nowhere pierced. The four occupants of the car emerged unscathed.

"Only a direct hit from a bomb or shell will knock these 'Tatanagars' in," went on the officer. "And as for shelling, they are the ideal thing, because if enemy guns register near us, all we have to do is to move some five hundred yards and the enemy gunners have to start all over again. And as for machine-guns, they hardly scratch the paint off the 'Tatanagars.'"

An Indian Army Observer with the Eighth Army reports that units possessing 'Tatanagars' swear by them. "Many stories have been told me," he writes, "of how 'Tatanagars' saved the lives of men under shell-fire and bombing. Indian craftsmen can be proud of their 'Tatanagars.'"

(From a Press Note issued by Inter-Services Public Relations)

ISSUED BY THE TATA IRON & STEEL CO., LTD. HEAD SALES OFFICE: 102A, CLIVE STREET, CALCUTTA.

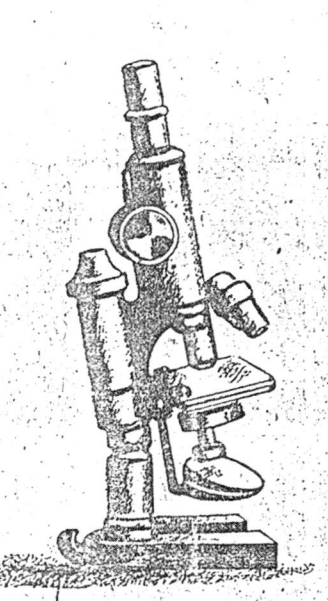

WHETHER IN THE LABORATORY OR IN FIELD OF BATTLE IT IS STEEL WHICH HELPS MAN IN HIS FIGHT AGAINST DEATH AND DESTRUCTION

BURN SCOB STEEL
THE STEEL CORPORATION OF BENGAL LTD.
12, MISSION ROW, CALCUTTA.

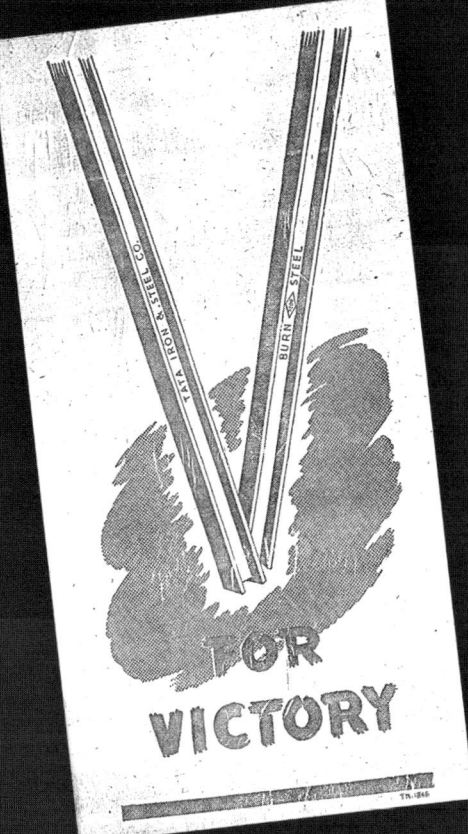

A news report by the API prompted a testimonial advertisement on armoured steel produced by Tata Steel that was used in the Tatanagar armoured cars.

The V for Victory advertisement was quite obvious when the war ended!

COMPETITION RESULT

THE TATA IRON & STEEL COMPANY, LTD.,

announce herewith the result of the competition for trade-mark designs held during July and August of the present year.

FIRST PRIZE
Is awarded to Mr. Saeed, Bhopal House, Lalbagh, Lucknow—Rs. 150.

SECOND PRIZE
Mr. E. A. Chary, No. 1, Mohan Bhuvan, Dadar, Bombay —Rs. 75.

THIRD PRIZE
Mr. Deo Dass J. Shetty, 1st year of Commercial Art Section, Sir J. J. School of Art, Bombay—Rs. 25.

We want to take this opportunity of thanking all entrants for their enthusiastic participation, which has demonstrated the talent available in this country. Designs which have not been awarded a prize will be returned at the earliest possible date.

TATA

ISSUED BY THE TATA IRON & STEEL CO., LTD.

In the year 1940 another unique idea was set in motion. An advertisement was decided to be created by the people for the people! The company chose to elicit creative ideas for slogans and by-lines from anybody with a creative flair. For this it released an advertisement announcing a competition with prize money for winners. Later in the year another advertisement was released to announce the winners.

COMPETITION

THE TATA IRON & STEEL COMPANY, LTD.

offer Rs. 250 in prizes for Trade Mark Designs suitable for incorporation in stationery, press advertising and publicity material in general.

1st Prize Rs. 150 **2nd Prize Rs. 75**
3rd Prize Rs. 25

Conditions:

1. This competition is open to professionals and amateurs.

2. Awards will be made by a jury consisting of the Principal of the Government School of Art, Calcutta, the Publicity Manager of the Tata Iron & Steel Co., Ltd. Calcutta, and the Manager of the J. Walter Thompson Co., (Eastern) Ltd., Calcutta.

3. The Tata Iron & Steel Co., Ltd., reserve the right to withhold awards if none of the designs is, in the opinion of the jury, of a sufficiently high standard. Alternatively, they reserve the right to make additional awards if the jury considers more than three designs are worthy of such recognition.

4. All prize winning designs will become the copyright property of the Tata Iron & Steel Co., Ltd.

5. The subject of the design is "TATA STEEL". A short qualifying slogan may be added such as "Strength—Security", or "A Sign of Strength".

6. Designs must be in black and white line, boldly executed to permit of considerable reduction in block-making if necessary.

7. Drawings should not exceed 3¼" in height and 2¼" in width.

8. Designs must bear the name and address of the entrant at the back and reach the Tata Iron & Steel Co. Ltd., (Publicity Department) 102A, Clive Street, Calcutta, by August 31st, 1940. The envelope should be superscribed "Design".

9. No responsibility can be accepted for any entries lost, mislaid or delayed, but every endeavour will be made to return rejected designs.

10. No correspondence can be entered into with competitors.

11. Awards will be announced in this newspaper and several others by September 30, 1940.

12. The decision of the jury is final in all matters relating to this contest and entries are only accepted on that understanding.

Along with the communication specific to the contributions by the company in supply of steel for the war efforts, the company also released advertisements in the leading dailies and journals on its supply of steel for domestic consumption and its continued endeavour towards building India.

These were the years when a bridge over the river Hooghly was being built. This structure promised to be a distinguishing feature on the Calcutta (Kolkata) skyline. About 85% of the steel used to build this structure was supplied by Tata Steel. On the first anniversary of the inauguration of the bridge the company released another advertisement that detailed the specifications and data of steel supply.

The 'Men of Steel' campaign was one of the most famous corporate campaigns of its time. It was a pioneer in the chapter of communications where a campaign spoke to the internal as well as the external stakeholders. This thought provoking campaign put on a pedestal a new breed and generation of men called the 'Men of Steel'.

By now the name and the address line of the company read as 'The Tata Iron & Steel Company Limited' but the writing style of the word TATA had been accepted in a block form akin to what it is now.

MEN OF STEEL 4.
In mammoth steel works, strong bearded men from distant Baltistan villages handle intricate machinery, assisting India to develop her vast industrial resources.
These artisans, experienced in the making of fine steel, form a new generation in India, proud of their designation—Men of Steel
ALWAYS EVERYWHERE STEEL FOR STRENGTH
TATA STEEL
ISSUED BY THE TATA IRON & STEEL CO. LTD., HEAD SALES OFFICE: 102-A, CLIVE STREET,

MEN OF STEEL 5.
Stalwart Sikhs from the Punjab are key-men today, in the unfamiliar surroundings of modern steel works.
Single handed, lifting sheets of red hot steel, they pilot them deftly through intricate machinery, from which they finally emerge as ships plates or as roofs of village homes.
These men form part of a splendid new generation in India—Men of Steel.
ALWAYS EVERYWHERE STEEL FOR STRENGTH
TATA STEEL
ISSUED BY THE TATA IRON & STEEL CO. LTD., HEAD SALES OFFICE: 102-A, CLIVE STREET, CALCUTTA.

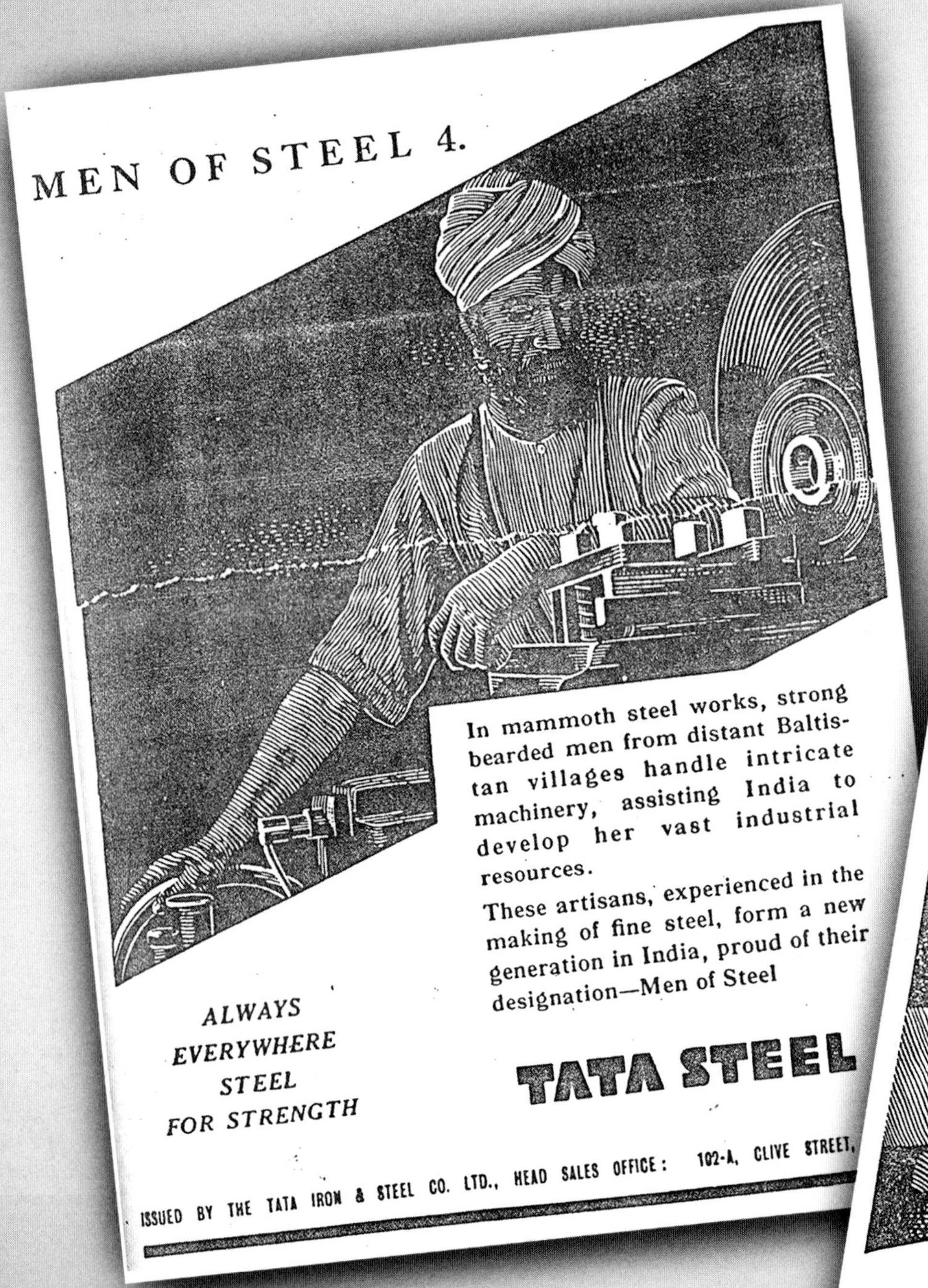

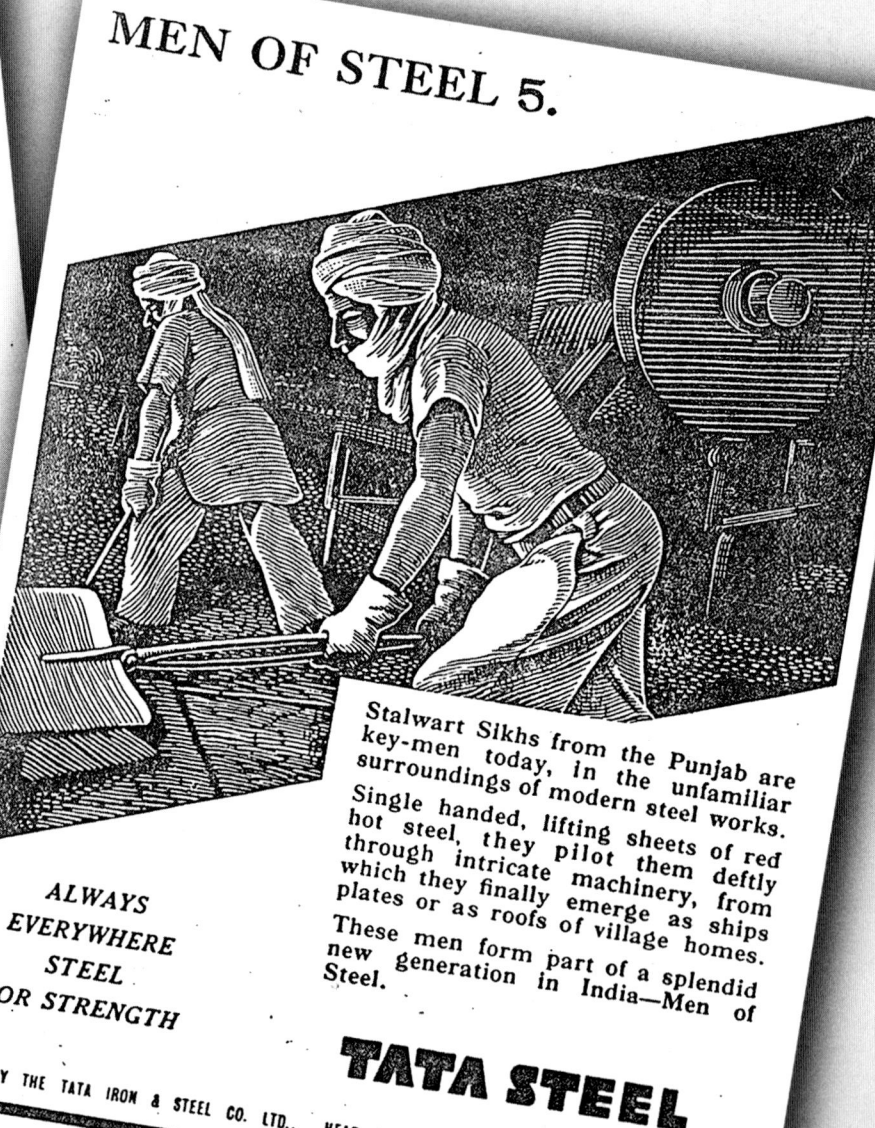

THE HAMMER

India's forges are busy now, for peace has brought a tide of extra trade.

In providing the simple but stout hammer for use in shaping fiery metal under the blacksmith's hand, the Iron & Steel Industry is putting its shoulder to the wheel of progress.

AGRICO TOOLS

Distributors for Bengal, Bihar, Orissa & Assam:
Messrs. Baboolall Singha & Co., 58, Clive Street, Calcutta.
Messrs. Gopeenath Paul & Sons, 210, Harrison Road, Calcutta.

Issued by the Tata Iron & Steel Co. Ltd.
(Agrico Department) Golmuri.

THE PICK-AXE

Do you realise how important is the construction and maintenance of roads and railways, to the commercial progress of this country?

Pick-Axes are simple tools but it is with their aid that improved railways and more and better roads are made.

In manufacturing these simple tools, the Iron and Steel Industry is doing all in its power to hasten the development of India.

AGRICO TOOLS

Distributors for Bengal, Bihar, Orissa & Assam:
Messrs. Baboolall Singha & Co., 58, Clive Street, Calcutta.
Messrs. Gopeenath Paul & Sons, 210, Harrison Road, Calcutta.

Issued by the Tata Iron & Steel Co. Ltd.
(Agrico Department) Golmuri.

THE SHOVEL

While digging deep beneath the soil in India's mines, or when preparing the earth's crust in readiness for building, the sturdy shovel is an indispensable tool for a tough job. We manufacture shovels in five different sizes. These are supplied complete with well-seasoned wooden handles.

AGRICO TOOLS

Distributors for Bengal, Bihar, Orissa & Assam:
Messrs. Baboolall Singha & Co., 58, Clive Street, Calcutta.
Messrs. Gopeenath Paul & Sons, 210, Harrison Road, Calcutta.

Issued by the Tata Iron & Steel Co. Ltd.
(Agrico Department) Golmuri.

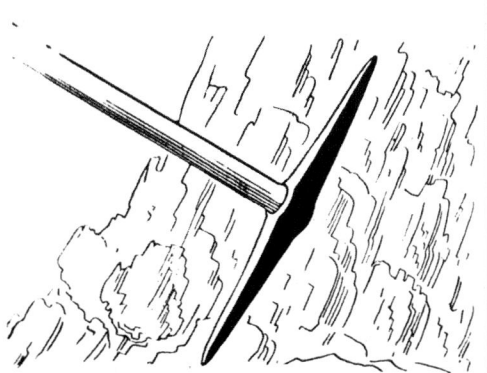

Tata Agrico

The Agricultural Implements Company Limited began manufacturing in 1922 with the introduction of pick-axes and shovels and other agricultural tools. However owing to want of sufficient finance for working capital and need for improvements in operations it was unable to make any headway. Tata Steel took over as the managing agency of The Agricultural Implements Company Limited in 1923.

The company released the first advertisement for the Agrico Division in 1927 and mentioned the product in all their general campaigns. It was however in the 40s that the product first enjoyed a dedicated campaign. This initial six part campaign had visuals of all the products and the body copy outlined their attributes. This campaign was followed by a series of other campaigns that continued till late 50s. By now the products were being exported to the neighbouring countries of 'Ceylon, East Pakistan and Burma'. These advertisements also appeared in many relevant trade journals.

The Building of a Nation

After a long struggle for freedom, India saw a new dawn on the 15th of August, 1947 as an independent nation. Just prior to Indian independence the company had contributed significantly to its product portfolio by successful experimentation and innovation. During the period of the war the company had set up new mills to meet the requirement of the railways and defence. Special alloy steels were produced that were the exteriors of the legendary 'Tatanagars'.

Tata Steel was now ready to meet the requirements of a new Nation.

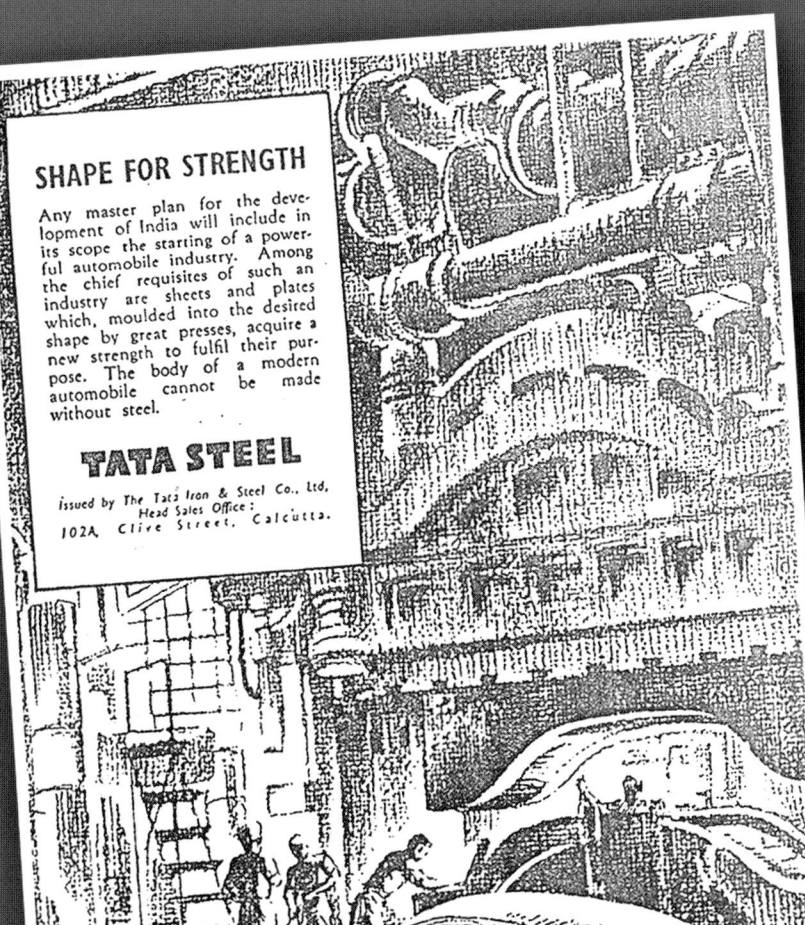

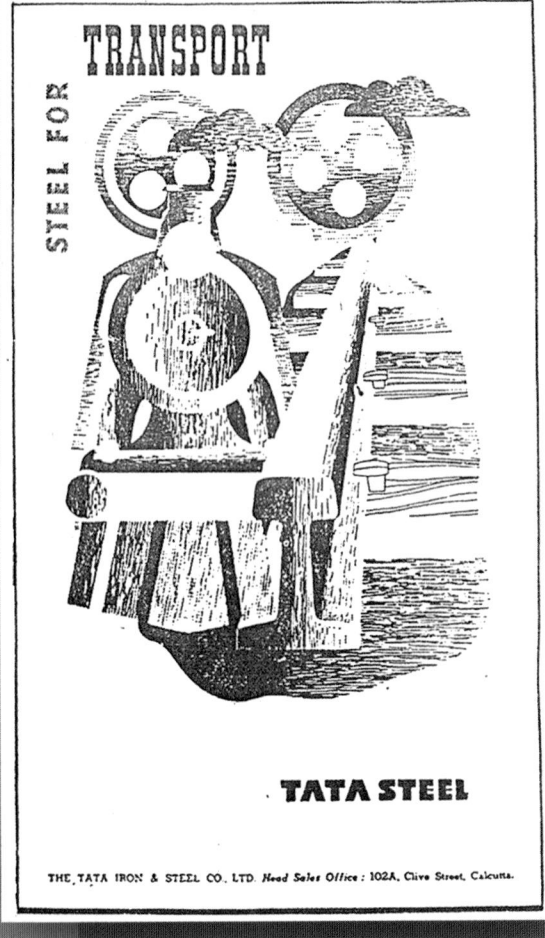
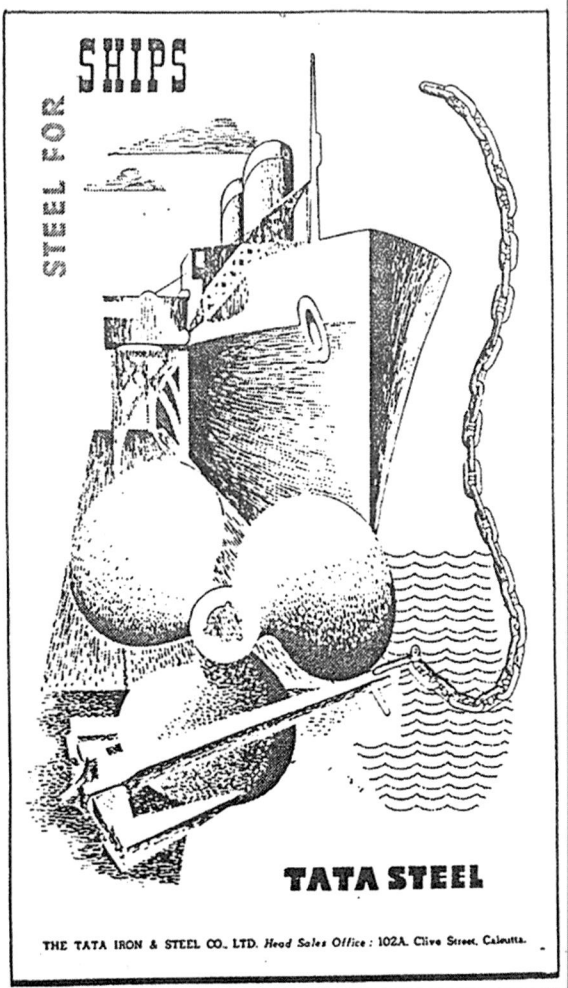

This pre-independence campaign stated, almost outlining the shape of things to come, the slogan 'Steel for Nation Building'.

The advertisements released post-independence were distinct from the earlier ones in terms of style. The headline 'Vision in Steel' conveyed the eagerness and hope with which the company anticipated India's future. This campaign touched upon the main aspects of nation building - from transport to agriculture to housing to medicine.

Leadership — *Our Ancient Heritage*

If Hippalus is blowing

By the 4th century A.D. when the Guptas set their capital at ancient Pataliputra, India was already a great maritime power.

As early as 275 B.C. when Asoka reigned, her seamen voyaged 60 days or more, in ever widening spheres of contact, and Indian merchandise was seen in the markets of Persia, Antioch and Alexandria.

In South India, the Port of Cranganore welcomed Arab and Roman merchants. Pliny speaks of a 40-day voyage to this port "If the wind Hippalus is blowing". These monsoon winds, discovered by Hippalus in A.D. 45 wafted trading fleets from the west to "Barygaza" "Soppara" and other ports in India.

Eastwards too, the seaways were alive with Indian trading fleets. As her influence spread, she enriched the neighbouring lands with her ancient wisdom and culture.

Today, Indian ships are once again on the highseas, carrying her merchandise to the markets of the world. In this Indian Renaissance, Tata Steel plays a vital part.

THE TATA IRON & STEEL COMPANY LIMITED

Leadership — *Our Ancient Heritage*

Centuries of ceaseless effort had taught the ancient Indian smelter the secret of producing steel of superb quality. To this, the artisan-designer added the exquisite patterns which had already made him famous. The craft and genius of these Indian artisans succeeded in fashioning articles of incredible strength and beauty which were carried in Indian ships to every known market in the civilised world.

So large and extensive was the Indian Steel industry that it produced in A.D. 415, a wrought iron pillar, which could not have been made anywhere else in the world until the 19th century. This pillar, 23 ft. high and weighing 6 tons, was erected by Kumara Gupta and was made with a technical excellence which continues to baffle scientists and engineers even up to the present day.

Stimulated by a resurgence of genius and determination, Indian craftsmanship is asserting itself afresh. In this Indian Renaissance, Tata Steel plays a vital part.

THE TATA IRON & STEEL COMPANY LIMITED

GENERAL PRESS

Peerless Ondanique

From early antiquity Indian Steel was famous in the civilised world. So greatly did Indian Steel excel all others that it was eagerly sought after wherever men met to trade. From "Wootz", as it was called in the Levant, was fashioned the famous chased armour of Damascus, as famed for its strength as for its beauty. The curved scimitars of the Saracens, chain mail and shining armour identical with that worn by the Knights of thirteenth-century Europe — these were made from the metal which the Indian master-craftsmen produced in their foundries.

The "Ondanique" Steel referred to by Marco Polo, the "Alhuide" and "Alfinde" of the Spanish armourers — these are but corruptions of "Hundwanij" — the Indo-Persian term for Indian Steel. Today, Indian craftsmanship and genius are expressing themselves anew. Ancient skill is equipping itself with new technology, to raise even higher our standards of excellence, and to gain new leadership. In this Indian Renaissance, Tata Steel plays a vital part.

THE TATA IRON & STEEL COMPANY LIMITED

GENERAL PRESS (India)

Leadership — *Our Ancient Heritage*

India's eminence in the Ancient World was due in great measure to the craft and invention of her artisans, the courage and resource of her mariners, the brilliance of her mathematicians and philosophers. Sanskrit literature and science, indeed, enshrined the vital nucleus of a great civilisation.

It was inevitable that powerful cultural influences would spread from these sources to the lands around her. Her philosophies, sciences and arts all took new root and flourished and such magnificent monuments as those of Boro Budur, Prabanam and Augor Thom testify to the energy and genius of Indian architects and builders.

Again, the influence of India's thought and culture is reaching outwards, speaking clearly and forcefully to the nations. Industrially, mighty projects are gaining the attention of the world, earning her a full measure of praise and appreciation. In this Indian Renaissance, Tata Steel plays a vital part.

THE TATA IRON & STEEL COMPANY LIMITED

Advertisements pivoting on India's glorious past were also released in the late 40s. This four series campaign was called 'Leadership, Our Ancient Heritage' and the base line was worded to emphasise how 'Tata Steel plays a vital part' in the renaissance!

yes, it is my plan!

Lights will be switched on in a thousand villages. Handlooms, lathes will hum and spin. Every small community will become the hub of a growing village industry. There will be work for everyone. The Five Year Plan provides for Rs. 127 crores to be spent on developing and adding to our power resources. Multi-purpose hydro-electric schemes will supply cheap power to industry. Here is proof of a nation's determination to take its place amongst the leaders of the world.

Lakhs of tons of Steel will be used to implement the many diverse projects of the Plan. And so, in numerous significant ways Steel will provide the foundations for a richer, more rewarding future for our nation and our people.

THE TATA IRON AND STEEL COMPANY LIMITED

"Five wonderful years! Time to build, time to create. For my child it will bring health, free schooling. For my family, security... may be, with hard work, a home to call our own!"

Nearly a quarter of the funds of the Five Year Plan will be used in increasing, improving and widening the scope of our Social Services. Rs. 425 crores will go to raising the standard of living of the people, training 13,000 new doctors, 20,000 new nurses and midwives. By 1956, more than 60% of all children over six years of age will be in our 2,02,142 primary schools. This long-range planning makes manifest our faith in the future. Here, indeed, is ...

a pledge to posterity

Lakhs of tons of Steel will be used to implement the many diverse projects of the Plan. And so, in numerous significant ways Steel will provide the foundations for a richer, more rewarding future for our nation and our people.

THE TATA IRON AND STEEL COMPANY LIMITED

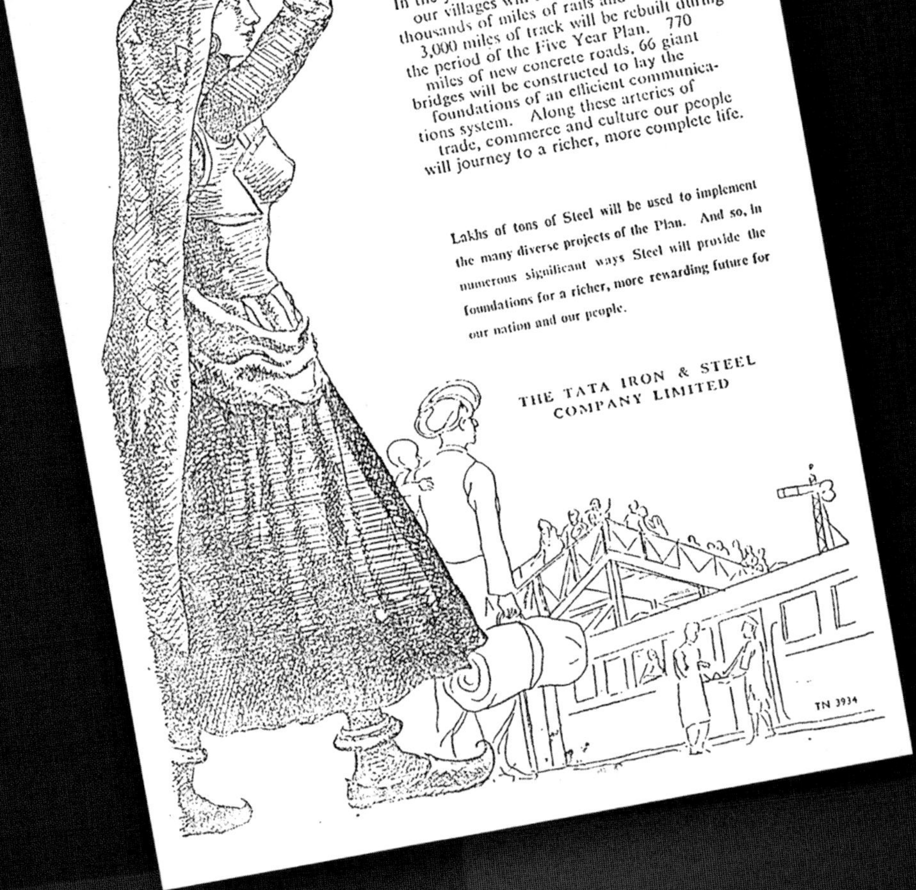
our villages
thousands of miles of rails
3,000 miles of track will be rebuilt during the period of the Five Year Plan. 770 miles of new concrete roads, 66 giant bridges will be constructed to lay the foundations of an efficient communications system. Along these arteries of trade, commerce and culture our people will journey to a richer, more complete life.
Lakhs of tons of Steel will be used to implement the many diverse projects of the Plan. And so, in numerous significant ways Steel will provide the foundations for a richer, more rewarding future for our nation and our people.
THE TATA IRON & STEEL COMPANY LIMITED
TN 3934

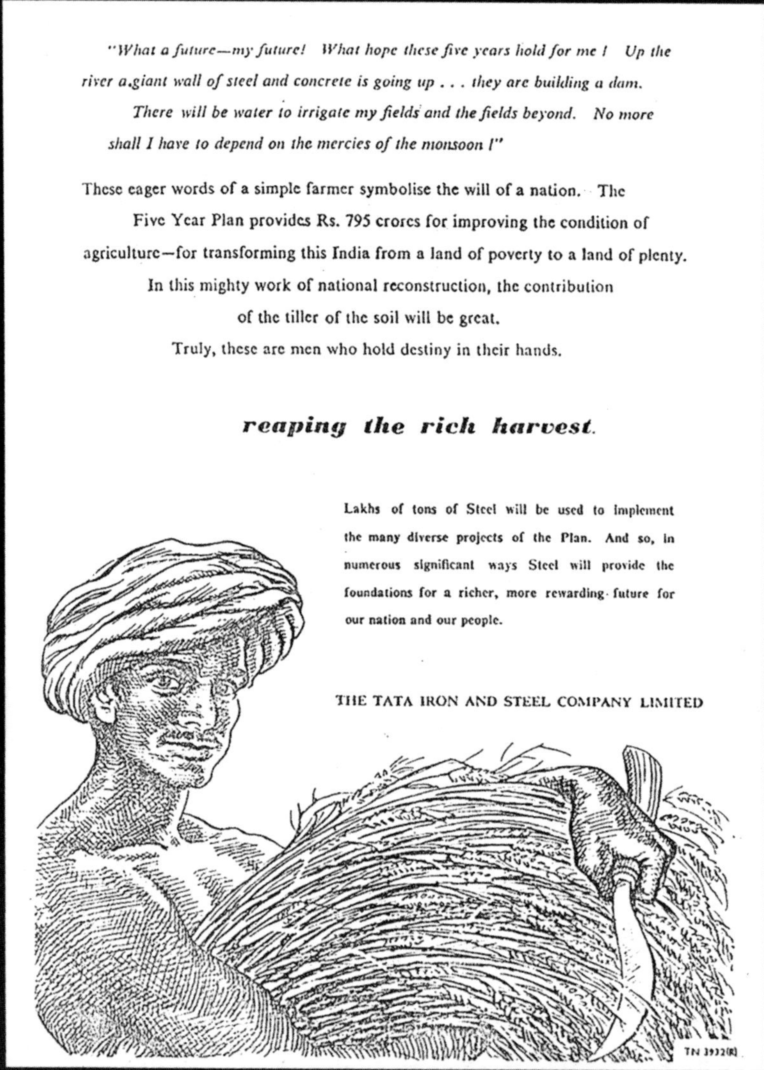
"What a future—my future! What hope these five years hold for me! Up the river a giant wall of steel and concrete is going up . . . they are building a dam. There will be water to irrigate my fields and the fields beyond. No more shall I have to depend on the mercies of the monsoon!"
These eager words of a simple farmer symbolise the will of a nation. The Five Year Plan provides Rs. 795 crores for improving the condition of agriculture—for transforming this India from a land of poverty to a land of plenty. In this mighty work of national reconstruction, the contribution of the tiller of the soil will be great. Truly, these are men who hold destiny in their hands.
reaping the rich harvest.
Lakhs of tons of Steel will be used to implement the many diverse projects of the Plan. And so, in numerous significant ways Steel will provide the foundations for a richer, more rewarding future for our nation and our people.
THE TATA IRON AND STEEL COMPANY LIMITED
TN 3932(R)

Five Year Plan had been announced by the
ak about how huge

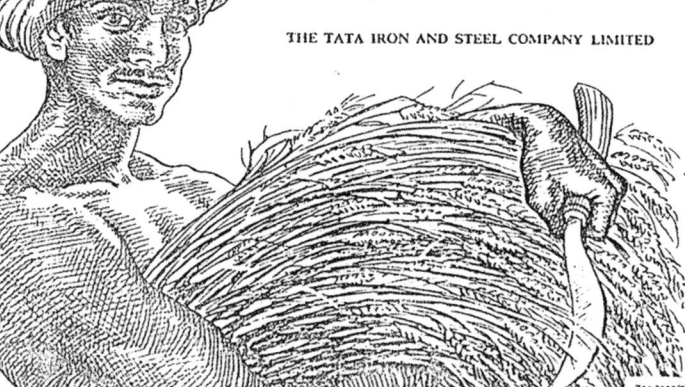

the vital factor in India's industri[es]

Within her womb the Good Eart[h]
crude and impure. Human effort
blast furnaces to smelt it into i[ts]
variety of finished products such
and sleepers. These steel produc[ts]
industrial strength.

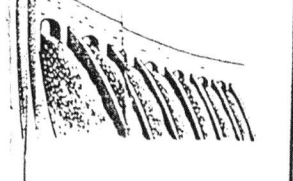

Power Projects... piling bars
and structurals for irrigation
and power projects.

Construction... beams,
les, channels, tees fo[r]
types of construction

Shipbuilding... steel plates made to Lloyd's specifications for shipbuilding.

TATA ST[EEL]

THE TATA IRON AND STEE[L]

TN.3639

progress...

...ls iron ore in its natural state —

...genuity bring this valuable ore to giant

...Complex processes transform the iron into a

...icturals and bars, sheets and plates, rails

...y a vital role in India's growing

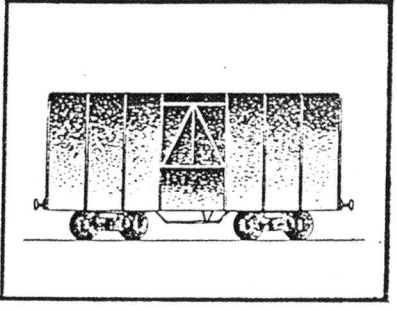

Railways ... rails, sleepers, fishplates, wheels, tyres, axles, etc. for railways.

...MPANY LIMITED

The zeal for nation building remained a core philosophy and the company released many single advertisements in the first few years after independence. The communication established the capability of the company and specific products that it offered.

These advertisements appeared in many trade related periodicals and in the general press.

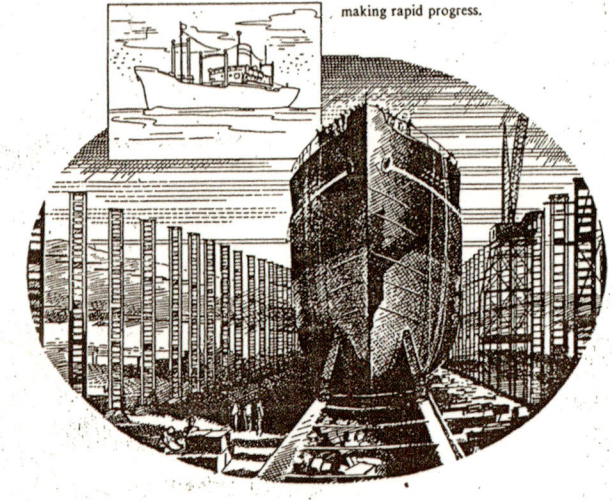

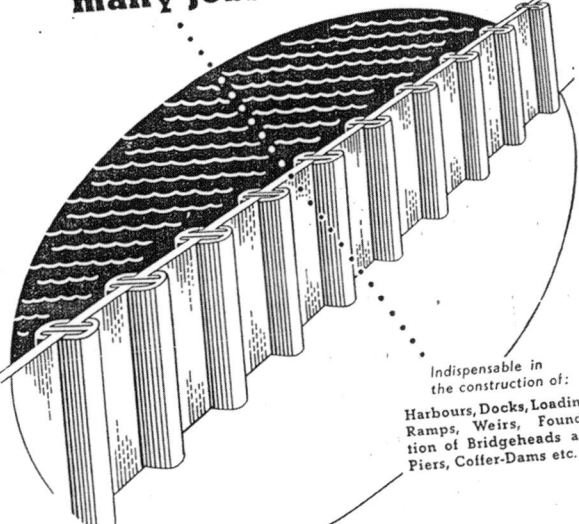

only steel piling bars can do so many jobs so well...

Indispensable in the construction of:
Harbours, Docks, Loading-Ramps, Weirs, Foundation of Bridgeheads and Piers, Coffer-Dams etc.

Steel piling bars are specified for major construction projects because they possess tremendous lateral strength and withstand great pressure. Giving perfect alignment they are easily adopted for corners, curves and circle work. Water-tight and resistant to corrosion, they are particularly suitable for safeguarding submerged construction against scouring and protecting river banks from corrosion.

...and in India steel piling bars are made by

Tata universal piling bars are being used in the nation's five most important development projects - Mor, Sarda, Ramapadasagar, Tungabhadra and Rasul.

THE TATA IRON & STEEL CO., LTD.
Sales Office:
23B, Netaji Subhas Road, Calcutta-1

TN-3349 This advertisement will appear in the General Press in India.
Advt. No. TN 3349 Prepared by :
Space : 9" x 3 Cols. J. WALTER THOMPSON Co.
August, 1952. (EASTERN) LTD.

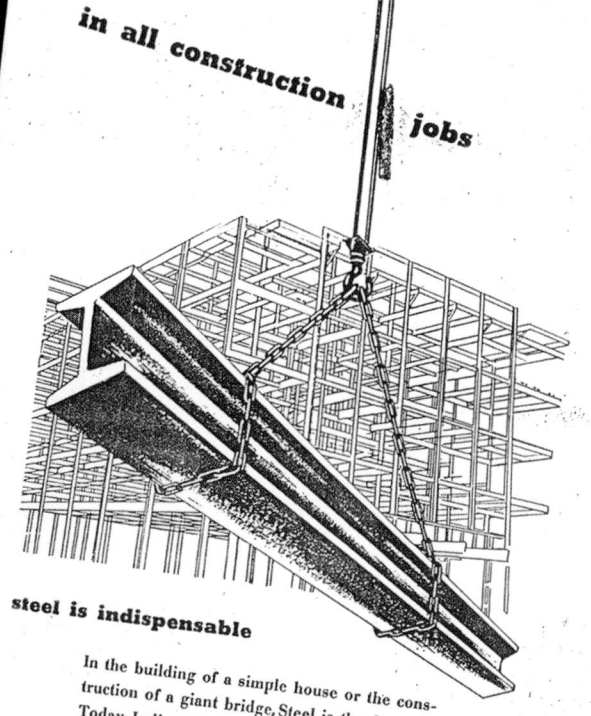

in all construction jobs
steel is indispensable

In the building of a simple house or the construction of a giant bridge, Steel is the first essential. Today, Indian Steel is making vital contributions to the nation's housing and communications projects by providing dependable heavy structurals. And during 1950-51, 73,000 tons of heavy structurals, were made of

TATA STEEL

THE TATA IRON & STEEL COMPANY LIMITED
23B, Netaji Subhas Road, Calcutta-1

TN-3350

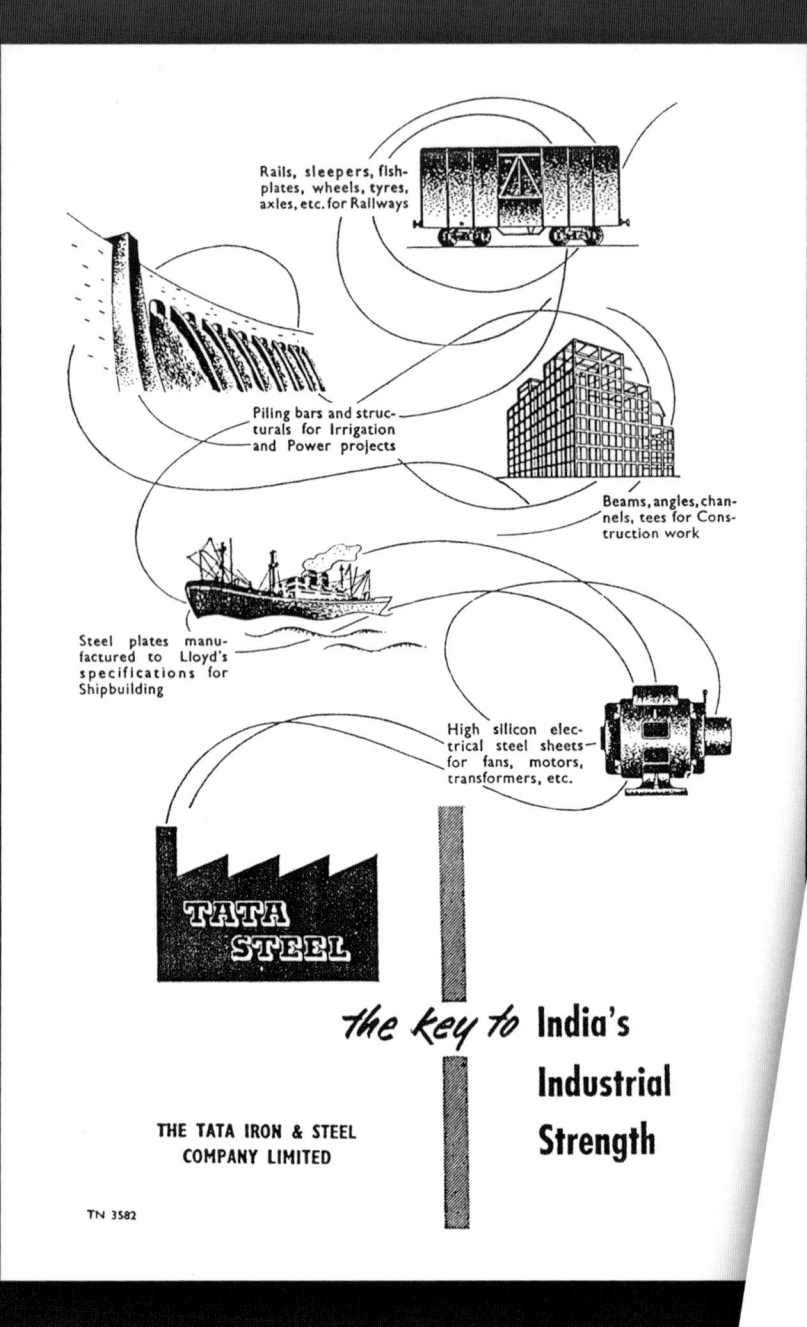
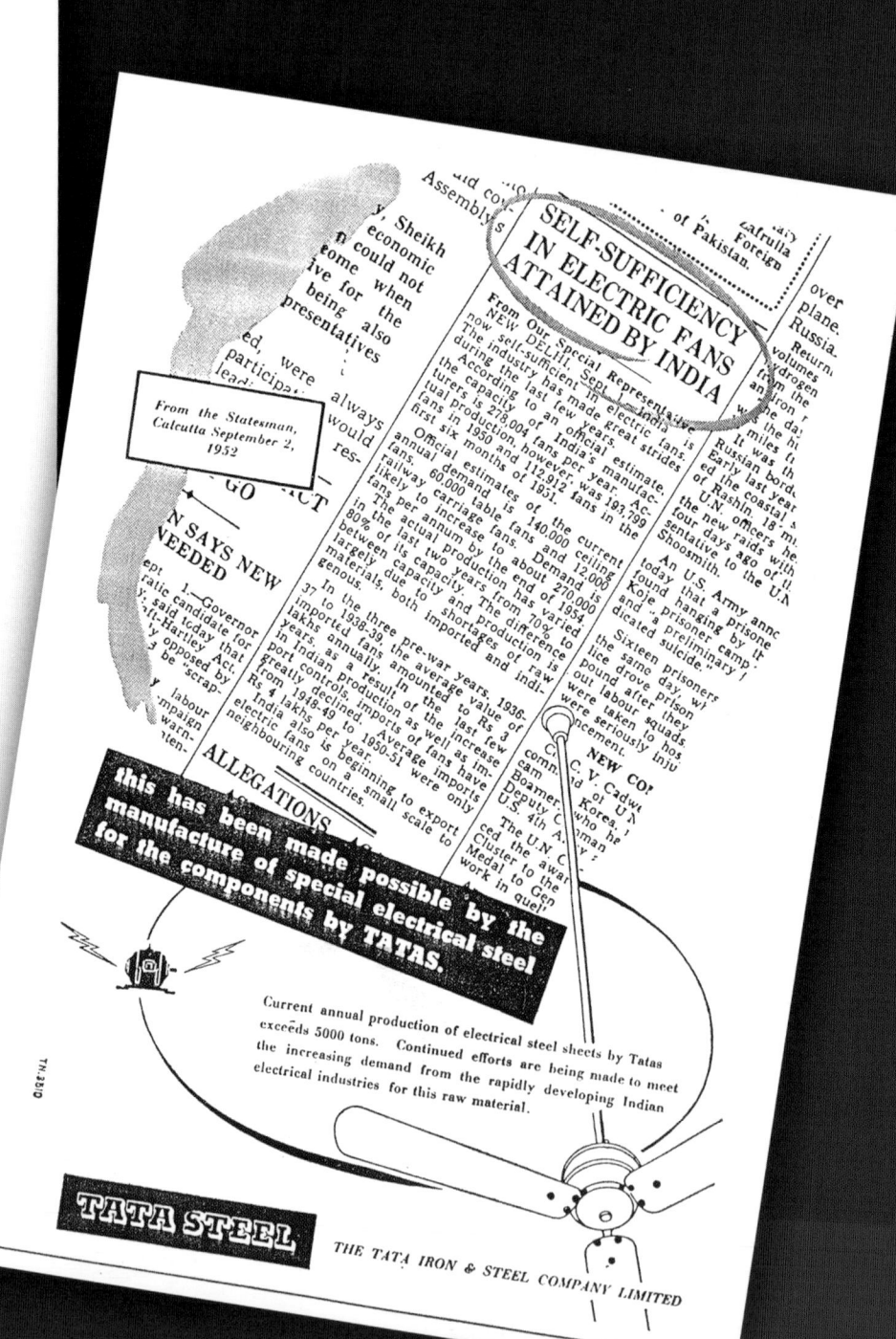

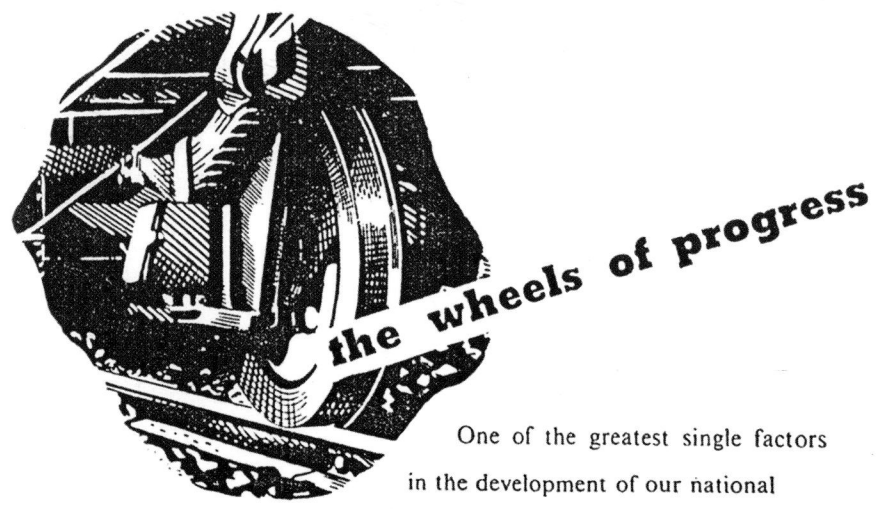

the wheels of progress

One of the greatest single factors in the development of our national economy is an extensive, efficient railway system. The smooth running of India's 34,000 miles plus of railroads is largely made possible by the supply of dependable railway materials made of Tata Steel.

move on paths of Steel

During 1950-51 the Indian Railways were supplied with 70,000 tons of rails and fish-plates, and 18,000 tons of wheels, tyres and axles made of

THE TATA IRON & STEEL COMPANY LIMITED
Sales Office:
23-B, Netaji Subhas Road, Calcutta 1

TH 3346

Tata Steel & Sports

Sports is a way of life in Tata Steel. The company released many special advertisements on the theme of sports.

A half-page advertisement was released in the general press wishing success to the members of the first Indian Olympic Team of independent India. There were also casual advertisements designed and released specifically for sporting events in the years that followed.

In the Two Million Ton (TMP) expansion programme the company designed and released a four part series titled 'Tata Steel Serves the Nation'. The creative idea was to use product profiles as sportspersons.

The advertisements were also not devoid of humour as established in these series on golf.

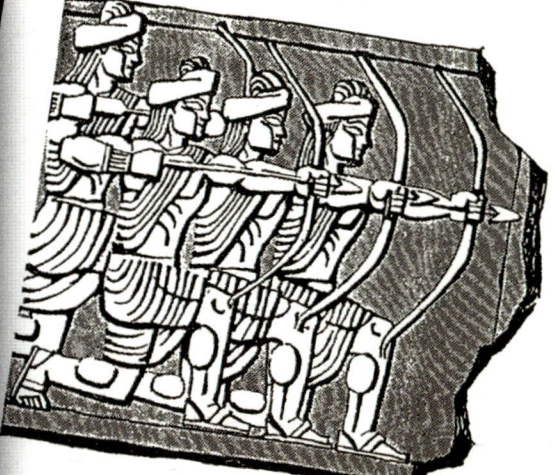

Two Million Ton Programme

With the approval from the first Five Year Plan, Tata Steel was ready to set in motion an expansion programme that would take the capacity of the plant to two million tons. With an initial fund of ₹ 100 crores from the Equalisation Fund the expansion programme was itself expanded to two million tons.

The initial advertisements that were released has the line 'Tata Steel serves the Nation'. The copy related how in the past steel from India had been used to craft weaponry, in the form of swords and arrow-heads, to win famous battles. The copy added that steel was still in the 'forefront of the country's thinking' and how the steel making capacity was being enhanced.

Many other advertisements were released during the construction period of the TMP to inform the stakeholders regarding the progress.

The green colour code

IN THE STEEL CITY OF JAMSHEDPUR, green is the colour code for top priority. At every desk, a green envelope or a green memo spells instant action for the stationery bears the legend: TWO MILLION PROGRAMME — IMMEDIATE.

Work goes on in an endless race against the clock with a daily stocktaking to assess progress. Every phase of operation is closely watched—from the manufacture of plant and equipment in three continents to work at the plant site, the ore mines and the collieries. Delays are at once spotlighted, whether in a distant Tokyo factory or nearer home on the rail route from Calcutta.

The project has already begun to yield results—two new 200-ton furnaces are producing the first additional steel under the Second Plan.

TATA STEEL
ON TO TWO MILLION TONS

Shovelling dolomite into a recently completed 200-ton furnace in the new Steel Melting Shop.

THE TATA IRON AND STEEL COMPANY LIMITED

The Last Phase

THE COMMISSIONING OF THE NEW Rs. 70-million Blast Furnace in Jamshedpur in October marks the beginning of the end of the expansion programme started in December 1955 to double Tata Steel's capacity to two million tons a year.

One of the largest in the world, the new Blast Furnace will produce 1,650 tons of molten iron per day. Completed earlier was the third Steel Melting Shop with its seven open hearth furnaces, which alone will produce 1.3 million tons of steel ingots a year. Also in operation now is the new Rs. 100-million Blooming Mill with a primary rolling capacity of two million tons.

Covering every phase of operation from the winning of ore to the rolling of finished steel, the expansion will be virtually completed by the end of 1958. The capital investment on expansion and annual replacements by Tata Steel over the five years 1955-60 is estimated at Rs. 1,330 million—more than one-fifth of the total outlay by organised industries in the private sector.

TATA STEEL
ON TO TWO MILLION TONS

The Tata Iron and Steel Company Limited

READY FOR FUTURE TASK

Early in January 1959, Tata Steel completed its two million ton expansion programme covering every aspect of operations from ore mining to the finishing of steel. Undoubtedly the biggest project undertaken in the private sector in the Second Plan, the expansion cost Rs. 95 crores and took only 3 years to complete. With teething troubles usual in bringing new plants into operation overcome, Tata Steel is confident of achieving full production soon.

As this phase of expansion comes to a close, Jamshedpur looks forward to playing its part in the task of the future.

JAMSHEDPUR
THE STEEL CITY

all hands on deck

THERE'S A RACE ON... A race against time for steel, still more steel to build a solid basis for a new, industrialised India. 1.3 million tons today, the target is 6 million tons by 1960! How much will it be by 1965?

Naturally, Jamshedpur is also in the race. Tata Steel is pledged to double its output to two million—and in two and a half years, too.

Tata workers and management have jointly taken up this formidable task. Their common determination to raise output inspires the recently signed Labour-Management agreement. In tune with the country's social outlook, this agreement accepts the principle of labour participation in management.

All hands on deck, Jamshedpur is steaming ahead full speed towards the finish.

TATA STEEL
SERVES THE NATION

TN 1038

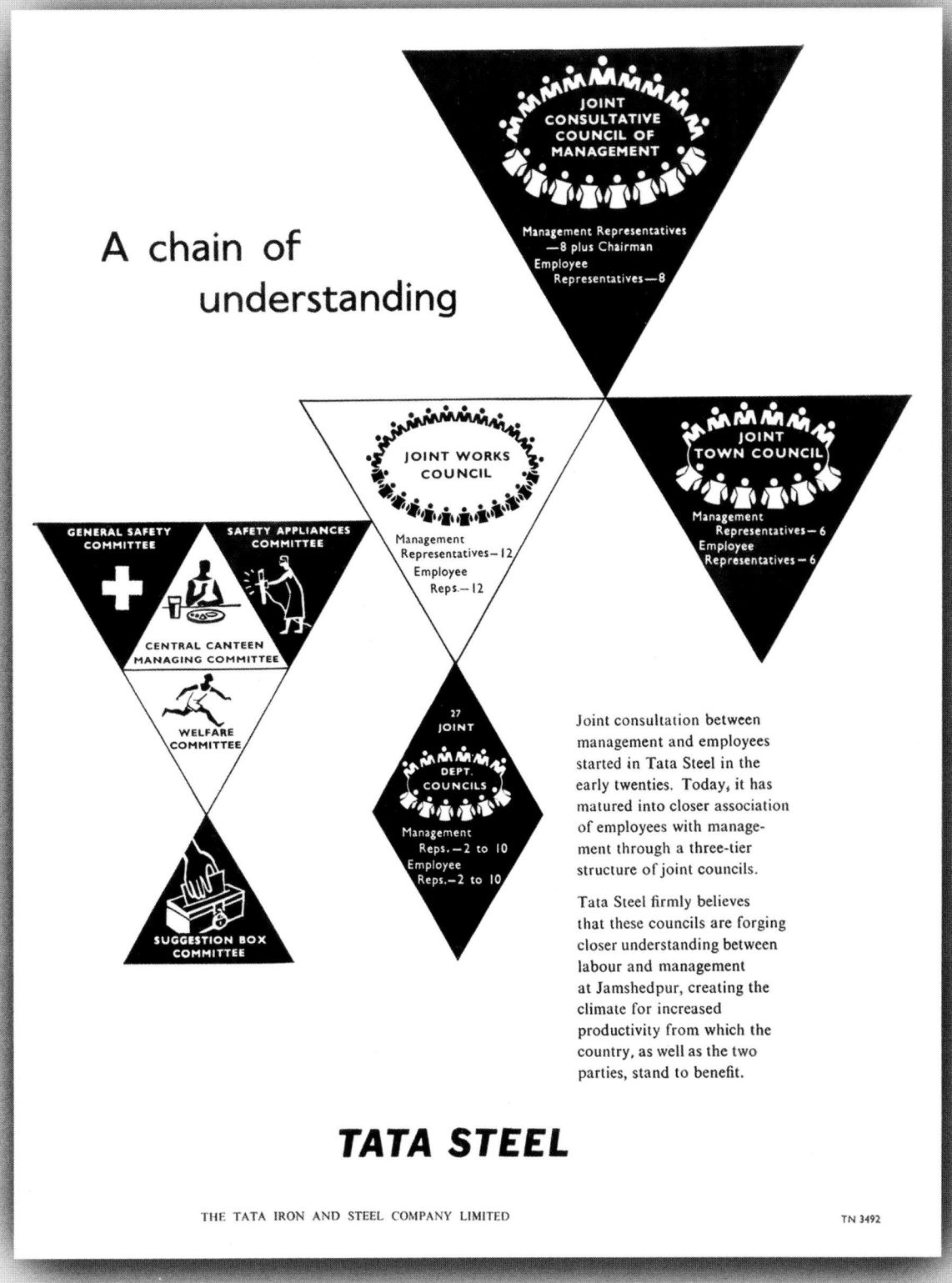

Joint Consultative Council of Management
Joint meetings between the employees and the management were in practice even as early as in the 20s. However a formal arrangement matured in 1956 with the introduction of the three-tier structure of Joint Consultations. Advertisements were released to announce this novel understanding.

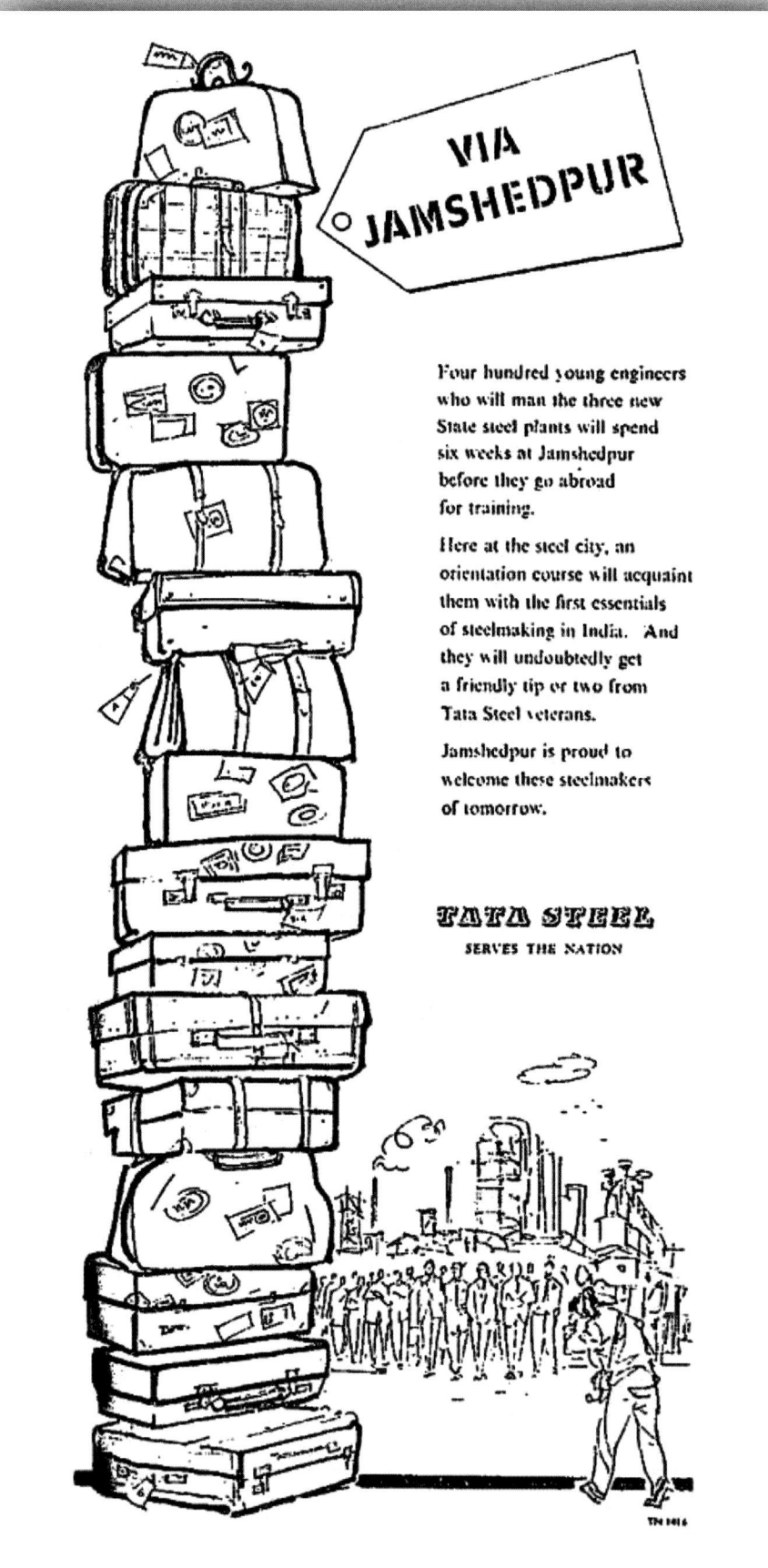

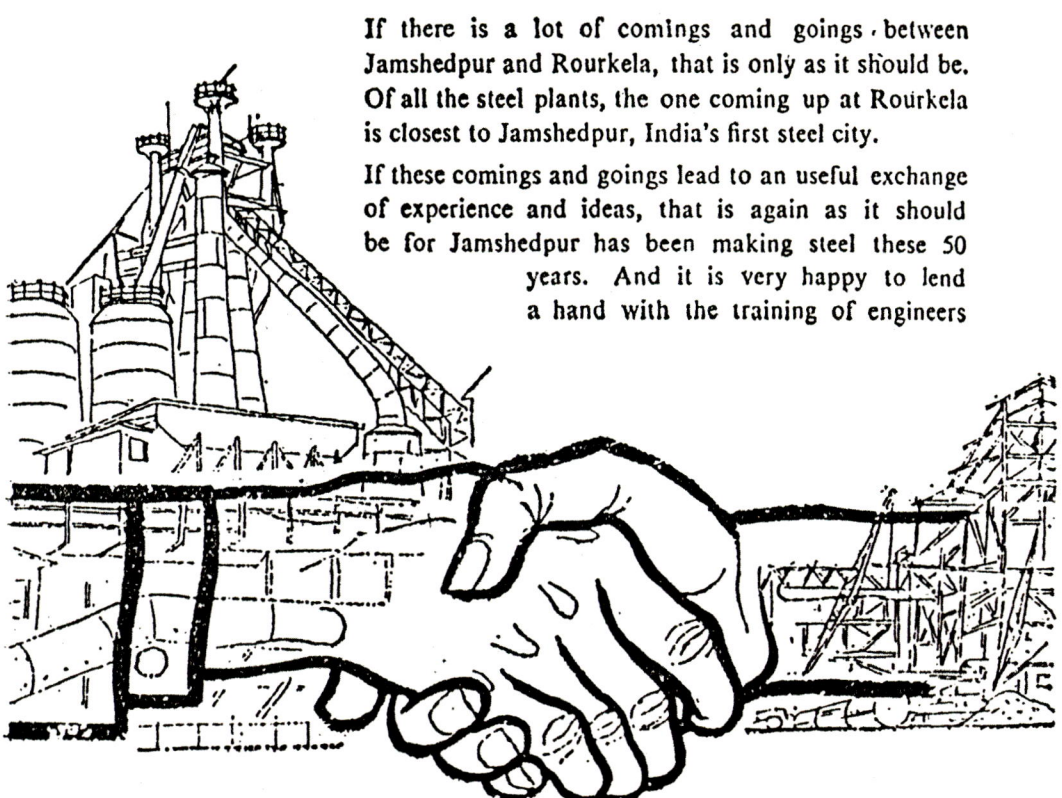

From a Neighbour

If there is a lot of comings and goings between Jamshedpur and Rourkela, that is only as it should be. Of all the steel plants, the one coming up at Rourkela is closest to Jamshedpur, India's first steel city.

If these comings and goings lead to an useful exchange of experience and ideas, that is again as it should be for Jamshedpur has been making steel these 50 years. And it is very happy to lend a hand with the training of engineers and technicians for Rourkela. There are nearly 150 of them at Jamshedpur—from key personnel to artisans.

Strengthening these ties of friendship are the surprisingly large number of old Jamshedpur faces that one sees at Rourkela. To them and their colleagues, Jamshedpur sends neighbourly greetings and good wishes.

Good Wishes to Rourkela

THE TATA IRON AND STEEL COMPANY LIMITED

SAIL

The company released two advertisements on the setting up of the steel plant in Rourkela. It welcomed this initiative by the government and promptly accepted the responsibility of training 150 of its engineers and technicians.

This advertisement drew praise from Mr. J R D Tata who congratulated the 'PRD' for it.

A founder of modern India...

in whose honour the Government of India is today issuing a special commemorative postage stamp

J. N. TATA
3rd March 1839 — 19th May 1904

In this year, which marks the 125th birth anniversary and the 60th death anniversary of Jamsetji Tata, we recall the gracious tribute paid by our much loved leader Jawaharlal Nehru, at Jamshedpur in 1958 on the occasion of the Indian Steel Industry's Golden Jubilee, to the Founder of the Indian Steel Industry:

"I have come here because the great steel works and the city of Jamshedpur have become symbolic of the growth of Indian industry... But the biggest reason of all is to pay homage to the memory of Jamsetji Tata... It is right that we should honour his memory, and remember him as one of the big founders of modern India."

TATA STEEL

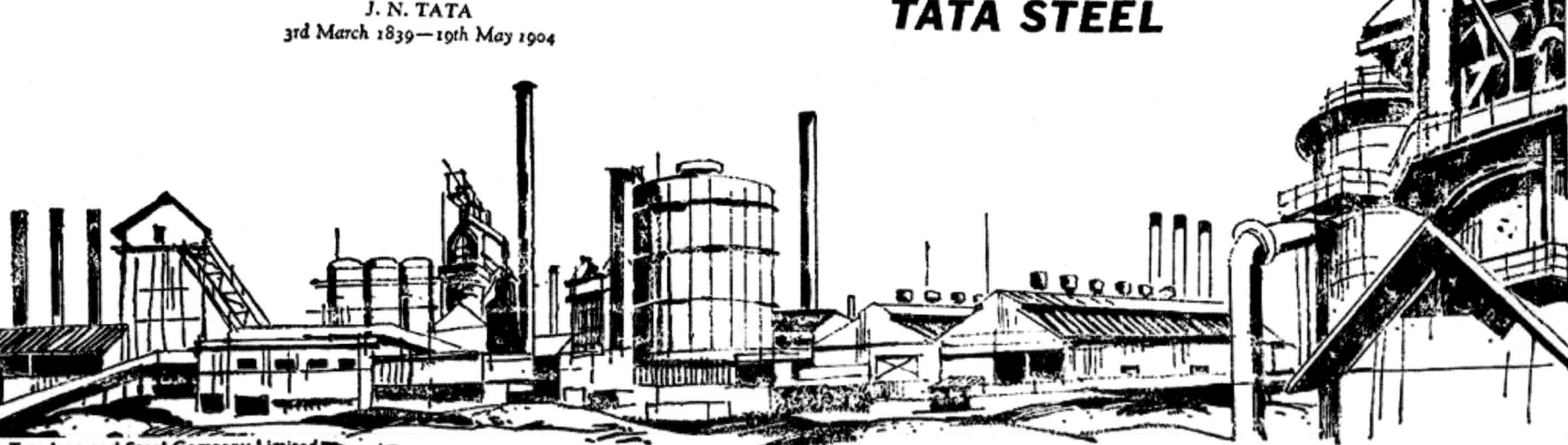

The Tata Iron and Steel Company Limited

50 years of Tata Steel

Tata Steel celebrated its Golden Jubilee in March 1958. The Jubilee Park in Jamshedpur was inaugurated by Prime Minister Jawaharlal Nehru. A special commemorative stamp and a First Day Cover were released by the Government.

The company released advertisements on the occasion but none of them spoke about the gift of the Jubilee Park to the City of Jamshedpur. Such was the modesty in communications!

50 YEARS OF TATA STEEL

FIFTY YEARS AGO A DREAM CAME TRUE. August 26, 1907, witnessed the fulfilment of the purpose to which Jamsetji Tata had devoted the best years of his life, the establishment of the steel industry in India. Over 8,000 Indians contributed Rs. 2 crores in three weeks to float The Tata Iron and Steel Company.

Four years later, the President of the Indian Mining and Geological Institute, referring to the "titanic enterprise" planted in what, a few years ago, was one of the wildest spots in India, said :

" . . . . In a few months it is expected that a fire will be lighted which will not be extinguished till the Gorumahisani hill has been melted into railway materials, beams, sheets, which will be so much material to open up this country, to traverse its rivers, house the people and to bring India forward into line with the most advanced of countries."

For fifty years The Tata Iron and Steel Company has served the nation.

In the jungle, where only a primitive village stood, it built a steel plant and a model town, which are the nation's pride. It has produced over 22,000,000 tons of steel, and Sakchi, a village unrecorded on the map in 1907, has become the city of Jamshedpur, the happy home of over a quarter of a million people.

A new challenge confronts Tata Steel today. In a race against time, work goes on round the clock at Jamshedpur to double the capacity of the Steel Works to two million tons per year, to contribute to India's future prosperity, and as enlightened free enterprise should, "to help to develop the people into props and girders of civilisation".

The Spirit of Adventure

"Tatas represent the spirit of adventure."
— Mahatma Gandhi

"Jamshedji Tata laid the foundations of heavy industry in India by starting Steel and Iron Works in, what came to be known as, Jamshedpur... It had a precarious childhood but the war of 1914-18 came to its help. Again it languished and was in danger... but nationalist pressure saved it."
— Jawaharlal Nehru
from The Discovery of India

Architects of India's steel industry. (from L to R) Jamsetji Tata, R.D. Tata, Ratan Tata and Dorabji Tata

"Be sure to lay wide streets planted with shady trees, every other of a quick growing variety. Be sure that there is plenty of space for lawns and gardens. Reserve large areas for football, hockey and parks. Earmark areas for Hindu temples, Mohammedan mosques and Christian churches."
— Jamsetji Tata to his son Dorabji, in 1902, six years before work started at Jamshedpur

"So far we have but scratched the surface of this great land. Vast resources still remain unexploited and unused in the service of man. To think that hundreds of thousands of people should ever fall at the touch of famine, or die from disease aggravated by insufficient nourishment, while there is so much latent food and wealth in the country! ...Is it not time to stir ourselves, to wake up to the great opportunity and the stern duty before us, the task of India's industrial regeneration?"
— Dorabji Tata addressing Tata Steel shareholders in 1918

"We are like men building a wall against the sea. It would be the height of folly on our part to give away any part of the cement that is required to make the wall secure for all time. That is why we and you have to use this money... to build up this great industry... And we should not think of dividends until we have done that...

"...Make no mistake about this point. We hold this money in trust for you. But you yourselves hold it in trust for the Indian Nation..."
— R. D. Tata addressing Tata Steel shareholders on June 4, 1925

"We are constantly accused by people... of wasting money on the Town at Jamshedpur. We are asked why it should be necessary to spend so much on housing, on sanitation and water-works, on roads on hospitals and on welfare. People who ask these questions are sadly lacking in imagination We are not putting up a row of workmen's huts at Jamshedpur: we are building a city..."
— R. D Tata addressing Tata Steel shareholders on October 25, 1923

The Indian Steel Industry celebrates its 50th Anniversary

THE TATA IRON AND STEEL COMPANY LIMITED

This advertisement will appear in English dailies throughout India on March 1, 1958

windows on the world

THE THREE UNIVERSITIES — Madras, Bombay and Calcutta — that opened in 1857 were like windows on the world. Through them flowed in a wealth of new ideas which struck at the roots of age-old apathy, of unquestioning acceptance.

One of the first to graduate from the Madras University was Sir T. Muthusami Aiyar (1832-1895), the first Indian judge of the Madras High Court. A liberal in thought, and yet firmly anchored to the finest in Indian tradition, Sir T. Muthusami worked hard to extend the benefits of modern education in South India.

Inspired by the example of Muthusami Aiyar and a host of other distinguished alumni, students go out today to fashion a new India... to banish illiteracy and spread knowledge... to heal pain and suffering... to smash atoms and weigh stars... to widen the frontiers of knowledge.

TATA STEEL SERVES THE NATION

windows on the world

THE THREE UNIVERSITIES — Calcutta, Bombay and Madras — that opened in 1857 were like windows on the world. Through them flowed in a wealth of new ideas which struck at the roots of age-old apathy, of unquestioning acceptance.

One of the first to graduate from the Calcutta University was Bankim Chandra Chattopadhyay, father of the Bengali novel. Vande-Mataram, his immortal invocation to the Motherland, shows that Western learning only deepened the poet's anguish and lent a fine point to his indignation.

Inspired by the example of Bankim Chandra and a host of other distinguished alumni, students go out today to fashion a new India... to banish illiteracy and spread knowledge... to heal pain and suffering... to smash atoms and weigh stars... to widen the frontiers of knowledge.

TATA STEEL SERVES THE NATION

Windows on the World

The company continued using the baseline of 'Serves the Nation'. In 1957 a three advertisement series was created to commemorate the Centenary Celebrations of the Universities of Madras (Chennai), Bombay (Mumbai) and Calcutta (Kolkata).

windows on the world

THE THREE UNIVERSITIES—Bombay, Calcutta and Madras—that opened in 1857 were like windows on the world. Through them flowed in a wealth of new ideas which struck at the roots of age-old apathy, of unquestioning acceptance.

One of the first to graduate from the Bombay University was Mahadev Govinda Ranade (1842-1901). Of this great jurist and thinker, C. F. Andrews said: "The most enduring aspect of the new reformation in India is linked most closely with the name of Justice Ranade".

Inspired by the example of Mahadev Ranade and a host of other distinguished alumni, students go out today to fashion a new India... to banish illiteracy and spread knowledge... to heal pain and suffering... to smash atoms and weigh stars... to widen the frontiers of knowledge.

TATA STEEL SERVES THE NATION

TN 1255

...the Press, the Press, the Press

to the eyes and ears of the nation

The King may issue his fiat
The Union its decree,
But the bubble is blown and the bubble is pricked
By Us and such as We.

Remember the battle and stand aside
While Thrones and Powers confess
That King over all the children of pride
Is the Press — the Press — the Press.

(after Kipling)

to the watchdog of our liberties

to the conscience-keeper of the community

greetings from **TATA STEEL**

TN 1183

Greeting the Fraternity

The company greeted the members of the print media and the advertising world by releasing advertisements either on the occasion of their annual sessions or special occasions.

The visuals and copy are self explanatory and speak volumes about the relationship that the communicators had with the press and the advertisement fraternity.

To our Armed Forces...

Twenty-five years ago a notable landmark in the history of India's Armed Forces was reached. The Military College, Dehra Dun, was founded in response to sustained national demand for higher military education in India. The Committee which drew up the concrete scheme for the College included Pandit Motilal Nehru and Mr. M. A. Jinnah.

On this anniversary, we gratefully recall the services of the College to the building up of our Armed Forces. Apart from their many duties at home, our Armed Forces today are helping to carry India's message of peace and brotherhood to distant lands and peoples.

Greetings from **TATA STEEL**

THE TATA IRON AND STEEL COMPANY LIMITED

Congratulatory Messages

From the mid 50s till the end of the decade many stand alone advertisements appeared in the trade and general press. These advertisements congratulated or lauded success.

The company wished the new session of the Lok Sabha and the Indian Armed Forces, it remembered Abanindranath and Ranjitsinhji, it greeted Chacha Nehru on his birthday and appreciated Rash Behari Law (one of its earliest shareholders). It also invited the citizens of India to visit Jamshedpur so as to 'give ... a sense of participation in India's growing industrial strength'.

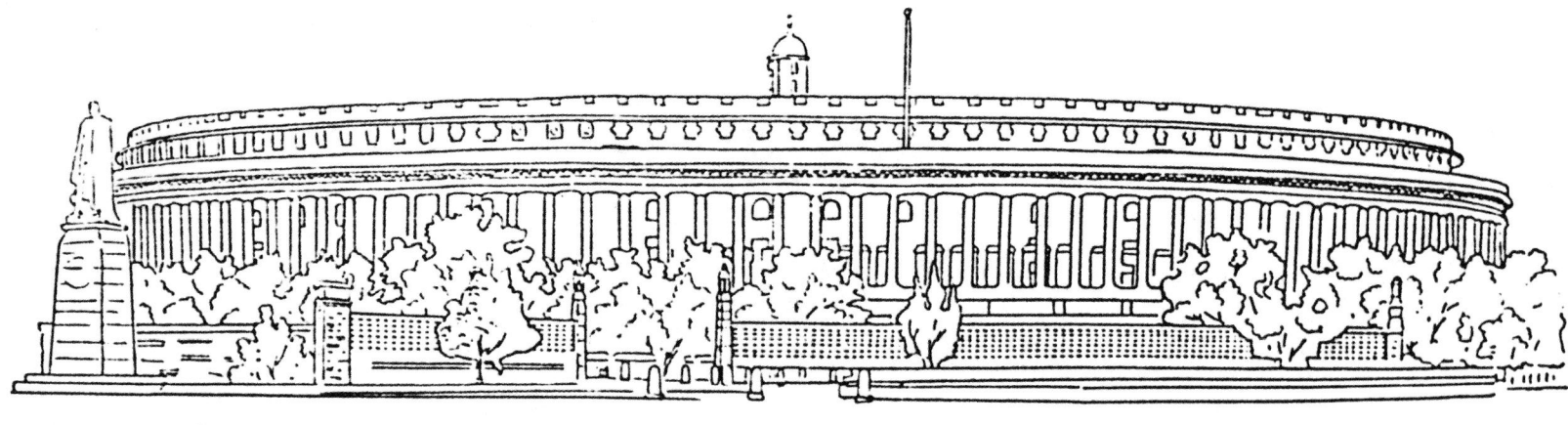

Greetings to the new Lok Sabha

"... a democrat must be utterly selfless. He must think and dream not in terms of self or party but only of democracy ..."

Mahatma Gandhi

TATA STEEL SERVES THE NATION

Homage to Abanindranath

Our homage to the memory of Abanindranath, leader of India's artistic renaissance, and the creator of a charmed world of winged words, unfading colours and deathless forms.

Abanindranath Tagore—painter, litterateur, aesthete. 1871—1951

THE TATA IRON AND STEEL COMPANY LIMITED

RANJITSINHJI

... the greatest of all

"... as a batsman pure and simple, Ranjitsinhji was unquestionably the greatest of all."
—*A. A. Lilley*

"Ranjitsinhji was a master of every stroke... To some extent he revolutionised the art of batting."
—*Sir Pelham Warner*

"Ranji is more than a batsman—he is nothing less than a juggler."
—*Clem Hill*

" 'e never made a Christian stroke in his life."
—*Ted Wainwright, quoted by Neville Cardus*

"Together, K.S. Ranjitsinhji and he (C. B. Fry) became an almost insoluble problem to those who bowled against Sussex."
—*R. C. Robertson-Glasgow*

"It is not in nature that there should be another Ranji. Did he really happen? or was he perhaps a dream, all dreamed on some midsummer's night long ago?"
—*Neville Cardus*

TATA STEEL

TN 3326

The Tata Iron and Steel Company Limited

men of faith

"From early morning till late at night the Tata offices in Bombay were besieged by an eager crowd of investors. Old and young, rich and poor, men and women, they came offering their mites; and, at the end of three weeks, the entire capital required for the construction requirements, £ 1,630,000 (over Rs. 2 crores), was secured, every penny contributed by some 8,000 Indians."

— Axel Sahlin

India's first venture into heavy industry, The Tata Iron & Steel Company, was thus launched on 26th August, 1907, with overwhelming support from investors and the public. Its growth into the country's largest single private enterprise and the principal steel producer was not without struggles and heartaches. In the 1920's when the very existence of the Company was at stake, there were many stout-hearted investors whose faith never faltered, and who cheerfully accepted the risks of a pioneering enterprise.

TATA STEEL

70-year old Mr. Rash Behari Law of 13-B Cornwallis Street, Calcutta-6, one of the first shareholders, who still holds stock in the Company.

THE TATA IRON AND STEEL COMPANY LIMITED

Balbir Singh, age 12

P. A. Rau, age 12

Ajita Datta, age 6

Greetings to Chacha Nehru

from the children
of
the Steel City

Three of the prize-winning entries in the Chacha Nehru Drawing Competition held in Jamshedpur Schools.

The Tata Iron and Steel Company Limited

Passing our way?

Do drop in on us at Jamshedpur... India's premier steel city. See how steelmen work and live. Drive through the sprawling 2-square mile steel works, now all set to produce two million tons of ingots a year. Watch molten iron flow out of giant blast furnaces, see it being turned into steel in the steel melting shops, and rolled into blooms and slabs, locomotive wheels, snaky skelp and sturdy structurals in the finishing mills. Take a side trip... visit the ancillary industries that make Jamshedpur the hub of Indian industry.

Walk along our tree-shaded avenues, relax in our famed Jubilee Park—a gift from Tata Steel to the people of Jamshedpur. Wherever you turn in this enterprising city, you will find things and men to interest you, to give you a sense of participation in India's growing industrial strength.

Drop us a line before you come... telegram to PROTATA, Jamshedpur, or letter to Public Relations Department, The Tata Iron and Steel Company Limited.

Jamshedpur

TATA STEEL

TN 3673

As part of the Two Million Ton Programme, the company set up a ferro-manganese plant in Joda. This advertisement was part of the series to inform the stakeholders of the status of the programme.

in a valley called Joda

Amid the silence of the Joda hills in the Keonjhar district of Orissa, a Rs. 17·5 million plant has gone into operation to produce ferro-manganese —a vital requirement in steel-making.

Served by an 18-mile rail link just completed, and power from Hirakud, this new plant starts with an initial capacity of 36,000 tons a year, to be stepped up by stages to 100,000 tons.

This plant has been speeded to completion eight months ahead of schedule, thanks to the invaluable assistance received from the State Government, the Hirakud Dam project and the Railways.

Life in the little-known village of Joda has turned a new chapter, reflecting the increasing importance of ferro-manganese as India strives towards a four-fold increase in steel capacity.

TATA STEEL
ON TO TWO MILLION TONS

Joda Ferro-Alloys Private Limited
(a subsidiary of The Tata Iron & Steel Co. Ltd.)

ement appeared in the General Press to mark the official opening of the Ferro-Manganese Plant, Joda, on 20th April, 1958.

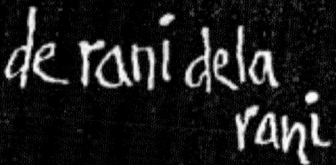

Two advertisements released using drawings by children. The message in the first one primarily focuses on encouraging local women to join the workforce. The words in the copy are lyrics of a local folk song.
The second advertisement drawn by seven year old Mitra, shows the predominance of steel in everyday life.

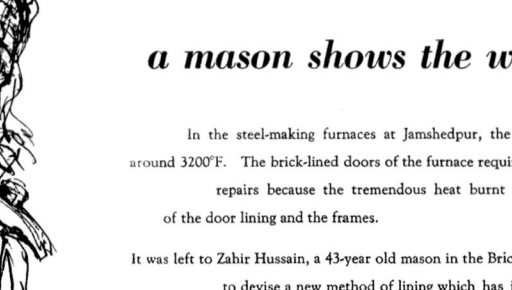

a mason shows the way

In the steel-making furnaces at Jamshedpur, the temperature is around 3200°F. The brick-lined doors of the furnace required frequent repairs because the tremendous heat burnt out the lower part of the door lining and the frames.

It was left to Zahir Hussain, a 43-year old mason in the Brick Department, to devise a new method of lining which has increased the life of the furnace doors. Zahir Hussain's achievement won him acclaim and a cash reward of Rs. 5,000—one of the 435 suggestion awards made since 1945.

This is one of the many examples of initiative from the shop floor benefiting the whole enterprise—another industrial tradition being laid in Jamshedpur, where industry is not merely a source of livelihood but a way of life.

JAMSHEDPUR
THE STEEL CITY

The Tata Iron and Steel Company Limited

the beginning of a tradition

FIFTY YEARS AGO, Sardar Pratap Singh Bhumra, now 87, was assembling cranes and electrical equipment as India's first steel works was taking shape in the wilderness of Chhotanagpur.

His son, Jwala Singh, joined the steel works his father helped to build. Drawing upon his mature technical skill, he suggested an improvement to soaking pit cranes which won him a reward from Management and appreciation from the American manufacturers.

Hari Singh, Jwala Singh's son, imbibed the family tradition early in life. A young electrician in Tata Steel's Skelp Mill, he was recently sent to Japan to study advanced crane maintenance.

Thus, a tradition of skill is being laid at Jamshedpur, where industry is not merely a source of livelihood but a way of life.

JAMSHEDPUR
THE STEEL CITY

The Tata Iron and Steel Company Limited

The Sixties and the Diamond Jubilee

The company was now producing two million tons of Steel and the city of Jamshedpur was now a thriving city with many modern facilities.

In the Fourth Plan expansion by Tata Steel by another million tons was approved by the Government. During this decade, associate companies such as TRF and TAYO were set up in Jamshedpur. The Government owned steel plants at Rourkela, Durgapur and Bhilai had begun production of steel as well. With this addition to the steel making facilities in India domestic production of steel had begun to cross the demand and a predictable fight in the markets was on the cards. The company celebrated its Diamond Jubilee in 1967 and gifted the city with an auditorium. In the special publication released for the Diamond Jubilee, Mr. J R D Tata wrote in his article 'Why..Tata Steel?'…. *the Tata Iron and Steel Company was conceived by Jamsetji Tata to put is country on the industrial map of the world. The conception naturally became a symbol of the Swadeshi movement. In the 60 years of its history Tata Steel has accomplished much of which it can be proud….Today it faces a new challenge which it must meet, remembering always its role as a pathfinder, its fundamental objective to serve the cause of India's industrial resurgence….'*

Amongst the first corporate campaign released in the beginning of the decade was a series called 'Jamshedpur - The Steel City'. This was a six part campaign which highlighted the aspects the working in the Tata Steel Plant and being a citizen of Jamshedpur.

49 years... not even a scratch

The rate of industrial accidents in India has increased from about 24 per thousand workers in 1938 to about 44 in 1959. Every year, over 93,000 workers are involved in accidents and 250 lives are lost. Also wasted annually are a million man-hours—enough to produce 170 broad gauge locomotives or 700 coaches for the Indian Railways.

Safety has always been Tata Steel's watchword as efficiency is hardly possible without it. 'No-accident month' as an annual feature, safety exhibitions, training in safety, safety awards, safer working conditions, a continuing campaign under the direction of joint councils to turn safety into a habit... these are some of the means adopted in Jamshedpur to prevent accidents in the Plant.

Safety, however, depends largely on the worker himself because about 75 per cent of industrial accidents are found to be caused by human negligence. This is where men like Jamuna Dube, the oldest employee in Tata Steel, come in. He has worked for 49 years without ever sustaining an injury, not even a scratch.

The importance of safety was one of the first things that Jamshedpur taught Dube when he arrived in the Steel City half-a-century ago... a city where industry is not merely a source of livelihood but a way of life.

JAMSHEDPUR THE STEEL CITY

The Tata Iron and Steel Company Limited

a day to remember

Fifty years ago today, the first ingot was rolled successfully on the blooming mill of the newly-started Tata Steel Works in Jamshedpur. The event evoked great enthusiasm as it marked the beginning of large-scale steel production in the country and the fulfilment of Jamsetji Tata's dream to give India a modern steel industry.

Since the rolling of the first ingot at Jamshedpur, the Indian steel industry has come a long way. From a target of six million ingot tons in the Second Plan to 10 million tons a year by the end of the Third Plan, the sights are being constantly raised. As Prime Minister Nehru said recently, the sky is the limit for steel production in a growing and developing economy.

JAMSHEDPUR THE STEEL CITY

The Tata Iron and Steel Company Limited

One who did not waver...

Jamshedpur's latest blast furnace needed a 'big bell'—a 20-ton component requiring highly skilled casting and machining. A difficult operation even if the right machine tools were available, but in 1958 they were not, and import seemed the only solution to all but one determined and resourceful young engineer, N. P. Naik.

Working on this problem in his leisure hours, Naik gradually crystallised his ideas into mathematical formulae and blue-prints. He developed, at the same time, a new machine tool to do the job by remodelling a small boring machine, stage by stage. Then started the casting and intricate machining, until, in a short time, Naik and his colleagues succeeded in producing a 'big bell', fully meeting the technical specifications to the last detail. As a tribute to Naik's fine endeavour, Tata Steel gave him an award of Rs. 10,000, the highest made under a ten-year old scheme to encourage initiative from the shop floor.

Men like Naik are carrying forward a fine Jamshedpur tradition, recalling Jamsetji Tata's exhortation: "Let the Indian learn to do things for himself."

JAMSHEDPUR
THE STEEL CITY

The Tata Iron and Steel Company Limited

...important beginnings

In December 1911, Bihar acquired the status of a separate province. This marked the dawn of a new phase in the history of this ancient state.

The birth of the new province synchronised with another epoch-making event. In December 1911, shattering the silence of the jungle hamlet of Sakchi, as Jamshedpur was then called, the newly-built Tata Iron and Steel Works roared into life and produced the first cast of pig iron. The commissioning of India's first iron and steel works helped to put Bihar on the industrial map of India and to set the country on the path to economic maturity.

In the course of fifty years, with the steel works as its nucleus, Jamshedpur has grown into a major industrial centre in India and the second largest city in the fast-developing State of Bihar...a city where industry is not merely a source of livelihood but a way of life.

A view of the Tata Steel Works in 1911

JAMSHEDPUR THE STEEL CITY

The Tata Iron and Steel Company Limited

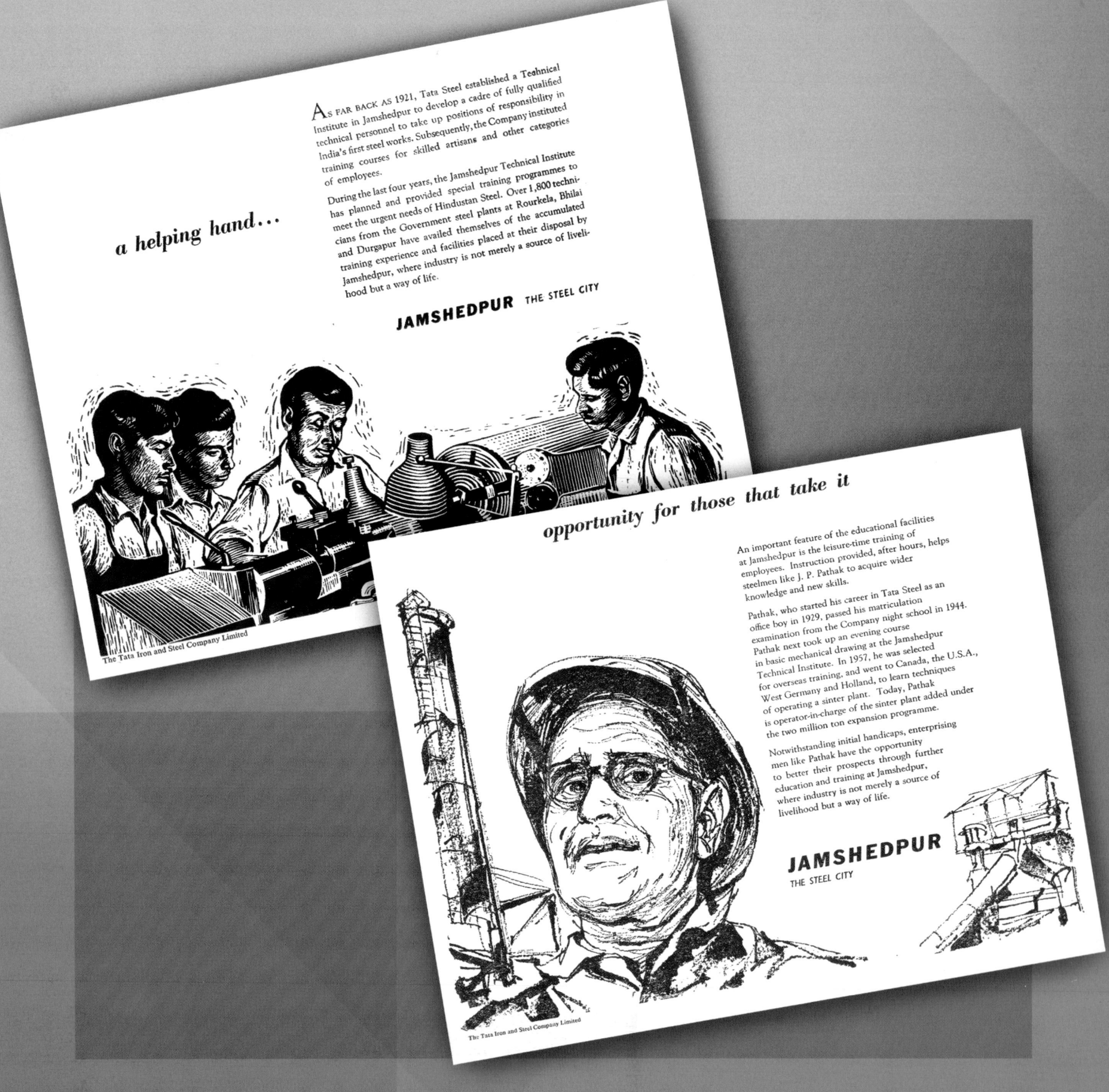

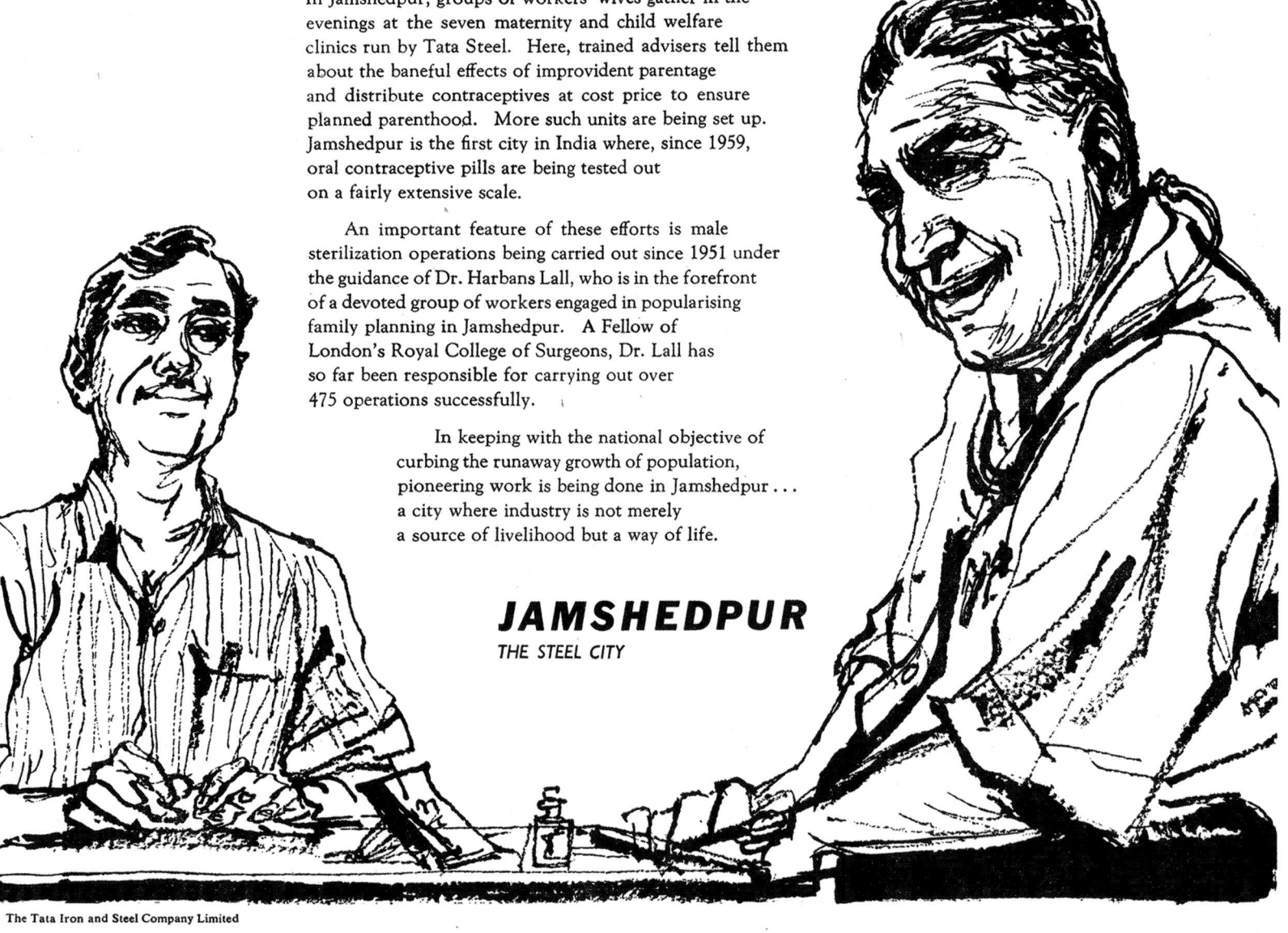

Quality control in steel

From 1st April 1965, Tata Steel have adopted the I.S.I. Certification marks scheme. Under this scheme, the steel plants take complete responsibility for the testing and certification of their products without the intervention of any outside authority. The Certification marks scheme in Tata Steel covers a wide range of products—structural steels in standard and ordinary qualities, billets for re-rolling, galvanised and black sheets and steels for general engineering purposes.

To implement the scheme, Tata Steel have expanded their existing facilities and inspection organization. All categories of steel are carefully followed through every stage of manufacture to maintain the highest standards of quality.

The adoption of the I.S.I. Certification marks scheme is yet another step in keeping with Tata Steel's basic objective—to supply steel products of proven quality to suit the customers' needs.

The Tata Iron and Steel Company Limited

With the view to be ready for the buyers market, the emphasis shifted to the production of special steels and new products. Quality had always been a hallmark in Tata Steel. In 1965 the company adopted the ISI certification. This was to further reinforce its commitment in producing steels to an accepted standard.

The Government also released a postage stamp and a First day Cover to commemorate the Founder J N Tata.

A founder of modern India...
in whose honour the Government of India is today issuing a special commemorative postage stamp

J. N. TATA
3rd March 1839 — 19th May 1904

In this year, which marks the 125th birth anniversary and the 60th death anniversary of Jamsetji Tata, we recall the gracious tribute paid by our much loved leader Jawaharlal Nehru, at Jamshedpur in 1958 on the occasion of the Indian Steel Industry's Golden Jubilee, to the Founder of the Indian Steel Industry:

"I have come here because the great steel works and the city of Jamshedpur have become symbolic of the growth of Indian industry... But the biggest reason of all is to pay homage to the memory of Jamsetji Tata...It is right that we should honour his memory, and remember him as one of the big founders of modern India."

TATA STEEL

The Tata Iron and Steel Company Limited

JAMSHEDPUR STEELMEN WIN SHRAM VIR NATIONAL AWARDS

R.C. BHAKAT
won top award of Rs. 2,000 for suggesting modifications to the New Floor Charger in the Plate Mill.

M.M. MAZUMDAR
won top award of Rs. 2,000 for suggesting use of basic bricks in door arches of open hearth furnaces.

BALWANT SINGH
won Rs. 500 for suggesting modifications to top coolers of open hearth furnaces.

K.B. DUBEY
won Rs. 500 for devising a gadget for protecting wagon brass-bearings from pilferage.

AFZAL HUSSAIN
won Rs. 500 for suggesting modifications to the side frame of L.B. wagons.

In March 1966, the Government of India held the first ceremony to honour the country's new heroes—technicians and industrial workers—with *Shram Vir* National Awards. These awards will be made every year in recognition of suggestions leading to higher production at less cost.

Of the 27 awards this year, no less than five, including two top prizes, went to Tata Steel employees—the largest number won by any industrial unit in the country.

At Jamshedpur, during the last 20 years, employees have put forward over 12,000 suggestions, of which nearly 1,000 have been accepted. These suggestions have helped to increase productivity and make operations safer, and have led to the utilisation of local know-how and materials for self-reliance.

Tata Steel is proud that it pioneered the Suggestion Box Scheme to encourage initiative from the shop floor...a scheme which is becoming a standard industrial practice in India today.

TATA STEEL

The Tata Iron and Steel Company Limited

The company congratulated the winners of Shram Vir Awards. These prestigious awards recognised the efforts of the workforce in the company.

The advertisement released on the occasion of the birth anniversary of the Father of the Nation in 1969.

Christopher Columbus! Now America has discovered us.

It's buying steel from us : 8,500 tonnes of ribbed reinforcing bars rolled to American specifications have been shipped to the USA. 61 years ago, America provided construction engineers to build our Steel Works : the first in India. Now firm orders already booked from the USA will bring in over a million dollars !

TATA STEEL

In the 1960s India was facing an acute shortage of foreign exchange. Tata Steel had been exporting Iron and Steel from its very first decade of production and responded to the need of the nation to contribute to foreign exchange earning by a thrust on exports to various countries including the USA!

Tata Steel goes abroad

Several times a year, ships carrying, among other things, angles and channels, bars and joists, and other steel products made in Jamshedpur, sail away from the Calcutta port… bound for East Africa, the Middle East, the Far East and Australia. These steel products are of utmost importance to the importing countries for their economic development.

Exports by Tata Steel, which are channelled through Commercial and Industrial Exports Limited (CIEL), the Government-recognised export house of the Tata Group, spurted to over 43,000 tonnes valued at Rs. 2.25 crores during 1966-67, from about 26,500 tonnes valued at Rs. 95 lakhs in the previous year. The increasing exports indicate Tata Steel's concern to do its bit to augment the country's foreign exchange earnings, so vital to the success of our national goal of planned industrialization.

TATA STEEL

TN 4018A

The Tata Iron and Steel Company Limited

When you're the first to see the need for a steel plant where only green plants grow, it's called vision.

Many years ago, Jamsetji Tata had a dream.

Of an India, not only politically independent but with its own strong economic and industrial system. Developed and worked by and for the people of the country.

A simple idea today, but uncommon for the India of the 1890's.

Then the vast coal and iron ore reserves lay forgotten, beneath tigered jungle tracts and centuries of unconcern.

There, the Tata man had to be athlete and explorer

 **TATA** [STEEL]

When you make it your business to help the best talent in the country get better, it's called enlightenment.

As far back as the 1890's Jamsetji Tata realised much of India's poverty was due to lack of opportunity.

The pioneering Jamshedpur Technical Institute, started in 1921, was just such an opportunity. Over the past fifty-three years it has developed for the nation a core of highly trained steel men, and some of India's finest technical managers, engineers and technicians for the public sector (Hindustan Steel, Bokaro Steel, the Heavy Engineering Corporation) as well as for the Tata Iron and Steel Company.

 TATA STEEL

When several thousand countrymen put their savings in your business, it's called <u>trust</u>.

It goes back a long way—to a time when the Tata Iron and Steel Company was being formed. Thousands of people, "some with stools and lunch boxes" lined up outside the Tata office to buy shares in the new Company.

Rich and poor alike subscribed.

And when it took just three weeks for some eight thousand people to raise 23 million rupees towards the new industry, Dorabji Tata wrote of this achievement with pride—"it was a purely Swadeshi enterprise, financed by Swadeshi money and managed by Swadeshi brains".

That was in 1907. Today at Tata Steel, this same spirit remains. The same pride that some seventy-five thousand people of India own shares in the Tata Iron and Steel Company —in a way that has now become the Tata tradition.

TATA STEEL

Seventies and Special Steels

The period saw the release of many specific subject advertisements that talked about the launch of new products that were required by a country preparing to meet the diverse demands of its fast emerging small, medium and large scale industries.

The new decade started with the release of a corporate campaign spread over three advertisements that spoke about the intangible assets of Enlightenment, Trust and Vision.

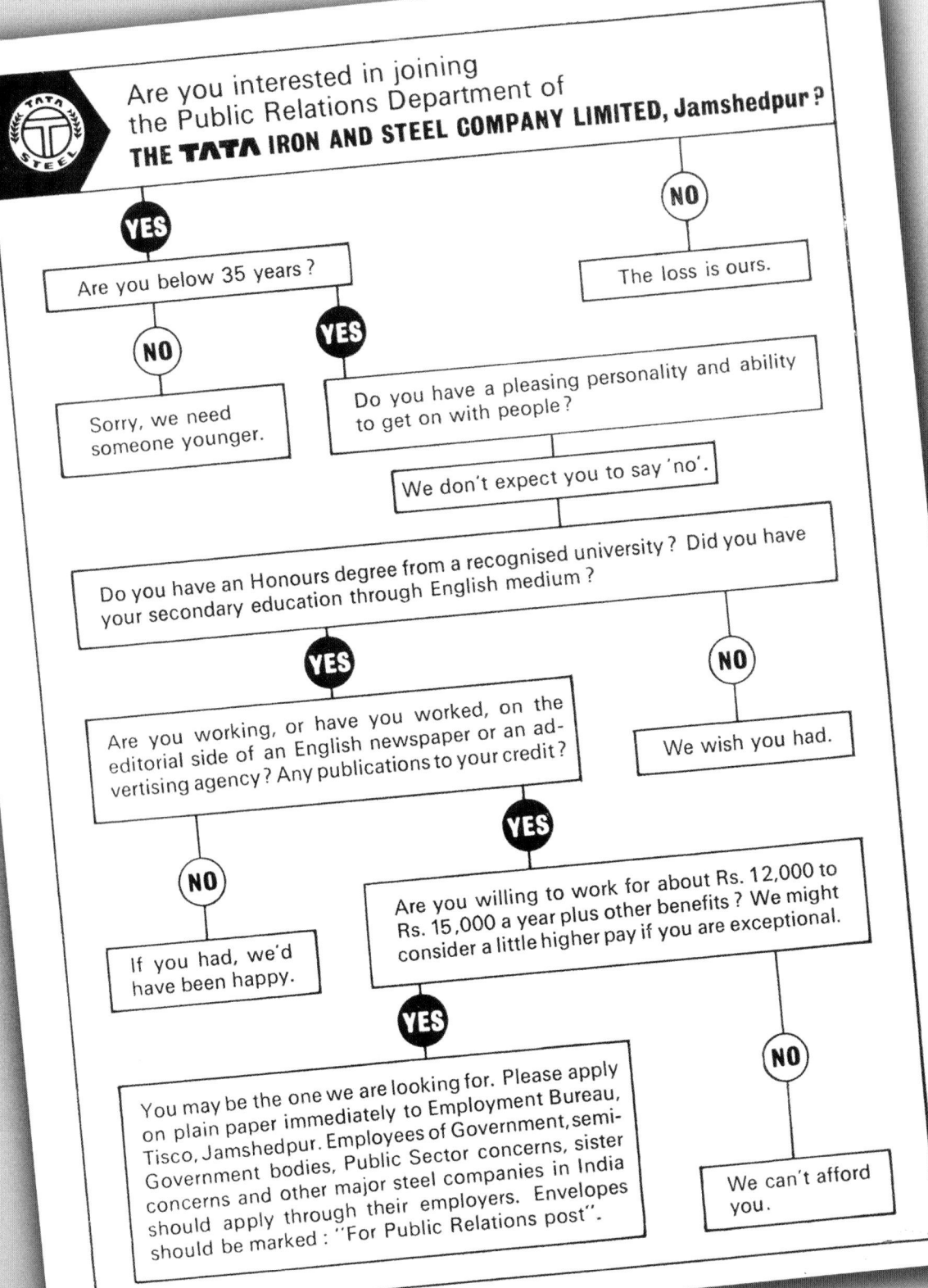

The company also released many statutory notifications and announcements including appointment advertisements. This unique appointment advertisement certainly caught the public eye!

You cannot hurt the plate if it's TISCRAL

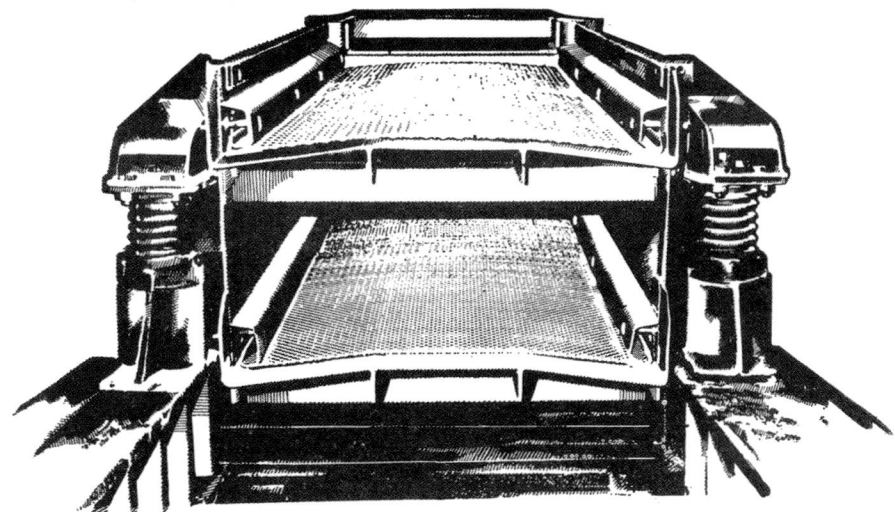

Core industries such as coal and steel are finding Tiscral plates ideal for bulk handling of iron ore, coal and sinter. Tiscral plates have found effective use in blast-furnace skip cars, screen plates, sluice gates, vibrating temping plates, hoppers, hammer-mills...wherever the going is rough and the threat of wear high.

Because of their exceptional wear-resistance, achieved through judicious alloying, Tiscral plates resist damage by scratching, grinding or gouging. The result is that replacements are needed less often, reducing downtime and expensive interruptions. Best of all, Tiscral blends toughness with ease of fabrication. It can be welded, machined, cut, punched and bent. Interested?

Please write for details to any one of the following:

- Director of Marketing
  The Tata Iron and Steel Company Ltd
  43 Chowringhee Road, Calcutta 700 071
- Joint Chief of Production Control
  The Tata Iron and Steel Company Ltd
  Jamshedpur 831 001
- Sr. Application Engineer
  The Tata Iron and Steel Company Ltd
  New India Assurance Building
  87 Mahatma Gandhi Road,
  Bombay 400 023
- Sr. Application Engineer
  The Tata Iron and Steel Company Ltd
  Bank of Baroda Building
  16 Parliament Street,
  New Delhi 110 001
- Sr. Application Engineer
  The Tata Iron and Steel Company Ltd
  20J Mahatma Gandhi Road,
  Bangalore 560 001
- Sr. Application Engineer
  The Tata Iron and Steel Company Ltd
  Park Centre, 24 Park Street,
  Calcutta 700 016
- Application Engineer
  The Tata Iron and Steel Company Ltd
  Indian Bank Buildings
  31 North Beach Road (3rd Floor)
  Madras 600 001

In the next ten years the company's communication dwelled more on its product mix and a series of product related advertisements that spoke about product specifications, customer benefits and applications.

The tough generation of high strength steel plates from Tata Steel

Tata LA-55 and LA-60: tough and economical

Tata LA-55 and Tata LA-60 are fine-grained, tough steel plates with excellent welding characteristics. Their better formability ensures freedom from cracking during fabrication. Tata LA-55 and LA-60 steel plates permit the use of lighter sections thereby reducing transport, handling and fabrication costs. Vehicles manufactured from these high strength plates can carry greater payloads because of reduction in deadweight.

Tata LA-55 and LA-60 plates are highly economical and suitable for heavy duty applications such as:

★ Earth-moving Equipment
★ Chain Conveyors
★ High-load Bearing Structures
★ Lightweight High Strength Bridge Components

For further details, please write to:

1. Director of Marketing & Sales, The Tata Iron and Steel Company Ltd
43 Chowringhee Road, Calcutta 700 071
2. Joint Chief of Production Control, The Tata Iron and Steel Company Ltd
Jamshedpur 831 001
3. Application Engineer (West), The Tata Iron and Steel Company Ltd
New India Assurance Building, 87 Mahatma Gandhi Road, Bombay 400 001
4. Application Engineer (North), The Tata Iron and Steel Company Ltd
Bank of Baroda Building, 16 Parliament Street, New Delhi 110 001
5. Application Engineer (South), The Tata Iron and Steel Company Ltd
20J Mahatma Gandhi Road, Bangalore 560 001
6. Application Engineer (East), The Tata Iron and Steel Company Ltd
Park Centre, 24 Park Street, Calcutta 700 016

If you were making aero engines you'd ensure reliability with our electro flux refined steel.

Enormous are the demands made on steels that make critical components ...high temperature steels and super alloys for aircraft, defence and space research; special steels for power plant turbine blades, discs and rotors; engineering steels for ball bearings, axles, cam and crank shafts; high speed steels, tool and die steels, shock resisting steels, heat and corrosion resisting steels; special steels for nuclear energy applications. Reliability must always be total in terms of strength, toughness and fatigue.

To make such extraordinary steel Tata Steel has developed, through its own R & D, India's first electro flux refining plant. Fully operative on a commercial scale, it produces steels of ultra high cleanliness, with minimum inclusions by way of size and numbers. It guarantees improved mechanical properties through controlled solidification resulting in fine grained structure with minimum segregation.

You now have a variety of special purpose steels for your type of industry, presented as ingots in sections 225 mm sq to 550 mm sq or equivalent section weighing up to 5 tonnes. For your requirements please write to any of the following.

■ Director of Marketing
The Tata Iron and Steel Company Limited
43 Chowringhee Road, Calcutta 700 071

■ Joint Chief of Production Control
The Tata Iron and Steel Company Limited
Jamshedpur 831 001

■ Sr Application Engineer
The Tata Iron and Steel Company Limited
New India Assurance Building
87 Mahatma Gandhi Road, Bombay 400 023

■ Sr Application Engineer
The Tata Iron and Steel Company Limited
Bank of Baroda Building
16 Parliament Street, New Delhi 110 001

■ Sr Application Engineer
The Tata Iron and Steel Company Limited
20J Mahatma Gandhi Road
Banglore 560 001

■ Sr Application Engineer
The Tata Iron and Steel Company Limited
Park Centre, 24 Park Street
Calcutta 700 016

TATA STEEL

Transmission line towers, cranes, skyscrapers, industrial structures, trucks, dumpers, trailers, ships, railway wagons, earthmoving equipment, offshore structures, underground structures for wells and mines, large span bridges, hangars, conveyor galleries, containers, high pressure gas transmission pipelines, giant storage tanks, pressed and formed components.

You make them better with Tata LA-50, LA-55, LA-60 and LA-60 (SMC)... a family of micro-alloyed high tensile steels.

The six major advantages they offer are:

Savings in fabrication, transport and erection costs.
Increased payloads because of lower dead weight.

Stronger structures.
Good formability.
Easy weldability.
Superior toughness.

For further information and your requirements, please write to any of the following:

Director of Marketing
The Tata Iron and Steel Co Ltd
43 Chowringhee Road
Calcutta 700 071

Jt Chief of Production Control
The Tata Iron And Steel Co Ltd
Jamshedpur 831 001

Sr Application Engineer
The Tata Iron and Steel Co Ltd
Bank of Baroda Building
16 Parliament Street
New Delhi 110 001

Sr Application Engineer
The Tata Iron and Steel Co Ltd
New India Assurance Building
87 Mahatma Gandhi Road
Fort, Bombay 400 023

Sr Application Engineer
The Tata Iron and Steel Co Ltd
20J Mahatma Gandhi Road
Bangalore 560 001

Sr Application Engineer
The Tata Iron and Steel Co Ltd
Park Centre
24 Park Street
Calcutta 700 016

Application Engineer
The Tata Iron and Steel Co Ltd
Indian Bank Buildings
31 North Beach Road (3rd Floor)
Madras 600 001

TATA STEEL

Two more special products from Tata Steel

Forged blanks and rolled rings in carbon and alloy steels for crane wheels and gears

Backed by over 65 years' experience in steel technology, Tata Steel introduces a range of sophisticated forged blanks and rolled rings for the manufacture of crane wheels and gears, which are far superior to those made by the conventional process of casting.

Forged blanks for crane wheels are manufactured from plain carbon steels. For gears, both forged blanks and rolled rings are available in plain carbon and alloy steels. All are suitable for thorough hardening, case carburising and flame hardening. A team of experienced engineers imposes rigid quality control measures at every stage of manufacture. Tata Steel forged blanks and rolled rings can also be supplied in rough turned, heat treated and ultrasonically tested conditions.

Tata Steel's forged blanks and rolled rings are available in the following ranges:

	Forged Blanks	Rolled Rings
Outer diameter	425mm to 1100mm	750mm to 2150mm
Width	115mm to 475mm	115mm to 180mm
	With or without pilot bore	Wall thickness 60mm to 100mm

Special consultancy service

Tata Steel's technical personnel offer their service and advice on the application of the forged blanks and rolled rings. For further details please contact:

1. Director of Marketing & Sales
The Tata Iron and Steel Company Ltd
43 Chowringhee Road, Calcutta 700 071

2. Joint Chief of Production Control, The Tata Iron and Steel Company Ltd, Jamshedpur 831 001

3. Application Engineer (West), The Tata Iron and Steel Company Ltd
New India Assurance Building
87 Mahatma Gandhi Road, Bombay 400 001

4. Application Engineer (North), The Tata Iron and Steel Company Ltd, Bank of Baroda Building
16 Parliament Street, New Delhi 110 001

5. Application Engineer (South)
The Tata Iron and Steel Company Ltd
20J Mahatma Gandhi Road, Bangalore 560 001

6. Application Engineer (East)
The Tata Iron and Steel Company Ltd
Park Centre, 24 Park Street, Calcutta 700 016

TATA STEEL

TATAVISION

Of what use are visionary ideas if they aren't communicated to the masses — electrifying them into action?

At Jamshedpur good ideas are seldom allowed to die through inaction. A dramatic example of this is the Family Welfare Programme.

Within three years of the start of the Programme in Jamshedpur, the number of people participating in Group Discussions shot up by ten times. And obviously discussions resulted in conviction: the birth rate in Jamshedpur began to decline in 1965.

What Tata Steel's Family Welfare Programme means to the people of Jamshedpur.

Two modern Urban Family Planning Centres plus six Maternity and Child Welfare Clinics give free contraceptives and advice on family planning.

Vasectomy operations are performed at the two Urban Centres and also at the Tata Main Hospital. For the Company's employees undergoing vasectomy, not only is the operation performed free, but a cash grant of Rs. 200/- is given in addition. As many as 1,650 vasectomies were performed between August and December last year. Cash incentives are also given to employees' wives undergoing tubectomy operations or loop insertions.

TATA STEEL

The Garden city 60 years ahead of its time

Jamshedpur, the steel city, is full of trees and flowers! In fact, it is one of India's most beautiful cities. And the amazing thing is that Jamshedpur was conceived and planned exactly as it is today, more than 60 years ago, long before planned cities became common even in the West.

Sonari — an underdeveloped area transformed. Under a phased programme, Tata Steel has helped the people to convert 20 underdeveloped areas into beautiful localities, with well-lighted roads and adequate water supply.

Jubilee Park. "Flowers, parks, and trees supply something which is, I imagine, of more basic importance to human beings and the human spirit than even iron and steel and it was a very happy thought to... provide this beautiful park."
Jawaharlal Nehru

The Tata Main Hospital. In addition to this well-equipped 600-bed hospital, Tata Steel has contributed to the setting up of an 82-bed TB hospital with a special children's ward.

Our strength is in our people as much as in our steel.

TATA STEEL

The city of Jamshedpur was now a modern place to live – an example for other new and old cities to emulate. The Green Steel City had many civic amenities which were coupled with care and welfare for its citizens.

1903. Braving jungles, intense heat and untold hardship, three intrepid pioneers set out on a voyage of discovery.

1907. At Sakchi the search ends. And India's industrial renaissance begins.

It was the culmination of a dream. And in its way an expression of the nationalist spirit. It was India's first steel mill 'built with Swadeshi money' as Jamsetji Tata had wanted it to be.

It was he who had sown the seeds: selected the technical experts, funded the project and provided inspiration and direction to his sons and associates. Now, four years after his death, the search had ended. But the early years had been rough, with disappointments and failures at every step. Still they had pressed on undaunted – Dorabji Tata, Weld and Saklatvala, the first of the intrepid pioneers, spurred on by the spirit of adventure. And in time came reward.

A chimney came up, a township started to grow. And men came from the cities, the towns, the villages – the first of the Tata Steel men. Soon the first ingot was rolled.

That was how Tata Steel was born – and Jamshedpur. By the endeavour of a fraternity of people aspiring, struggling and achieving. Today, Tata Steel is one of the country's largest and most progressive industrial enterprises – and Jamshedpur a city of opportunity. This is as Jamsetji Tata would have wanted it. For he firmly believed that the wealth which industry generates should benefit the people, enrich the nation.

1907-1982

What benefits the people, benefits the nation. **TATA STEEL**

As a part of the Platinum Jubilee Programme of Tata Steel, a series of seven advertisements were released. These advertisements recounted 'the fascinating saga of the country's first steel plant and celebrated the history of an organization and the remarkable spirit of its people who made it what it is today'.

100 cc - A Century of Communication

First and last–it's always been our people.

Well before the steel plant actually came up, the Founder, Jamsetji Tata, had listed labour welfare as 'one of the first cares' of the employer. For he firmly believed that by looking after the health and welfare of employees, we were laying the sure foundation of industrial harmony—and prosperity.

This concern for the well-being of the work force is reflected in the Company's endeavour to provide various benefits: 8-hour day (1912), Free Medical Aid (1915), Leave with Pay (1920), Worker's Provident Fund (1920),
Accident Compensation (1920) and Retiring Gratuity (1937). Most of these were introduced by Tata Steel for the first time in India many, many years before they were contemplated in the West and enforced by law in this country.

And all along the employee has responded in equal measure. Giving his all through the good years and the bad.

It is this sense of belonging, this fierce pride in the Tata name that has fostered over fifty years of industrial harmony in the Company—a unique record.

75 TATA STEEL 1907-1982

What benefits the people, benefits the nation.

> "...a museum piece that should charge visitors for the privilege of seeing its efficiency in operation."
> *A steel expert from Europe*

At 75, Tata Steel grows younger by the day.

Innovation and experiment. Concerted action. Resisting age and decay while improving efficiency. Producing to over 100% capacity, on an average, for the last eight years. That's how a 75-year-old keeps perennially young. Making every decade a passage of progress.

The modernisation programme now under way at Tata Steel seeks to go far beyond updating steel melting capacity. It takes into account the tremendous technological advancements in steel making. The need to develop human skills and productivity to that pitch. To place even greater reliance on research and development so that the emphasis of production shifts from quantity to quality, from simple steels to special steels—to meet the needs of modern industry.

These are the challenges of the years ahead. Challenges which Tata Steel will meet with determination, ingenuity and initiative.

It is this spirit of enterprise that has epitomised Tata Steel's operations throughout its 75 years. A spirit nurtured by the concerted efforts of a fraternity of uncommon people working towards a common goal—the resurgence of industrial India.

It is as Jamsetji Tata wanted it to be—an industry which would generate wealth to benefit the people and enrich the nation.

75 TATA STEEL

Founded August 26, 1907
1907-1982
TATA STEEL

What benefits the people, benefits the nation.

A Fusion in Steel

Indian Tube merges with Tata Steel

The Indian Tube Company Limited is now the Tubes Division of The Tata Iron and Steel Company Limited.

This amalgamation strengthens the Division and promotes efficient operation.
Its commitment to product reliability and customer service will continue as before.

The Tubes Division of Tata Steel reaffirms its responsibility towards its valued customers who have lent their support over the years.

TATA STEEL
Tubes Division
43, Chowringhee Road, Calcutta 700 071

The Branch Offices of the Tubes Division remain unchanged.

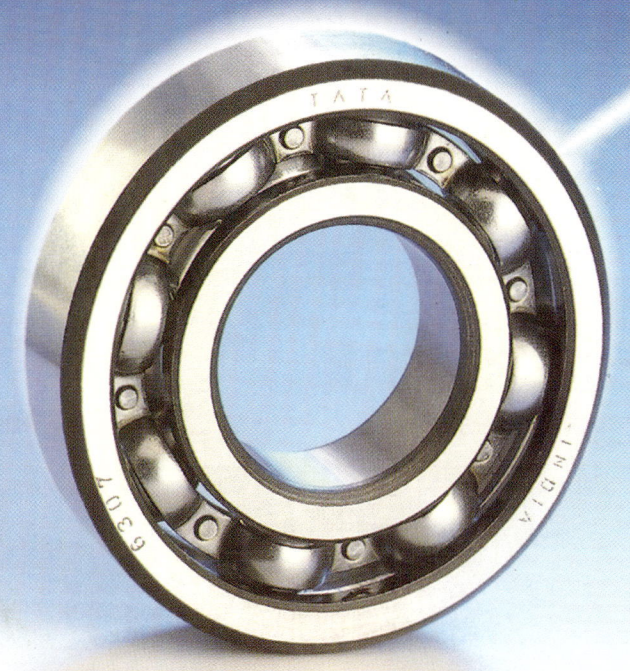

The early 80s saw the merger of the company with the Indian Tube Company. Tata Steel also acquired the Metal Box Bearings Unit in Kharagpur. These acquisitions became the Tubes Division and the Bearings Division of the company. General press advertisements were released to announce these takeovers and the addition of two new products of Tata Pipes and Tata Bearings in the list of products.

Tata Steel... the name that embodies a wealth of experience, gathered over 75 years of working under Indian conditions.

Tata Steel... the name that stands for an integrated system of production—from mining to finished products. No wonder, Tata Steel is so strong—in quality and reliability.

Tata Steel... the name that stands for innovation and progress—the driving force behind many a success story.

And, now, Tata Bearings... a great step forward from rings to precision bearings. Surely, the beginning of a new movement.

Yes, tomorrow's leader is here!

TATA BEARINGS
Born of steel... born to lead.

Tomorrow's Leader.
Born with the Strength of Steel

A Division of
TATA STEEL

'Mera Type... Tata Pipe'

Now easily available at affordable prices!

Tata Pipes are my type of pipes because they will last me a lifetime. Thanks to their higher steel thickness and additional zinc coating, I don't have to worry about the supply of water for my family or my crops.

Tata Pipes are now available upto 150 mm (6") n.b.; ever since the commissioning of Tata Steel's latest HFIW Tube Mill, designed by the world leaders, Kusakabe of Japan.

TATA PIPES | TATA QUALITY

TATA TUBES
A Division of **TATA STEEL**

When Madras Port Trust wanted liner plates that would save valuable equipment downtime

Ore silo at Madras Port Trust

they chose TISCRAL

TISCRAL. One and a half times more wear-resistant than mild steel plates.

The excellent performance of TISCRAL liner plates in ore bunkers at the Madras Port Trust convinced engineers at Kudremukh that TISCRAL is not only more durable, but also more cost efficient in the long run—because it reduces downtime and avoids expensive interruptions.

For them, the results are longer, smoother operations, fewer replacements and less maintenance. The same results will apply to your equipment.

More corrosion resistant than mild steel plates and easily fabricated at site, TISCRAL liner plates are used in the manufacture of a wide range of material handling/processing equipment. For core industries such as coal and steel. In cement, mining, metallurgical and road construction machinery and for vibrating screens. TISCRAL plates are ideal for bulk handling of iron ore, coke and sinter. In blast furnace skip cars; and in screen plates, sluice gates, hoppers and hammer mills.

For your requirements, please write to any of our sales offices or to
The Director of Marketing
The Tata Iron and Steel Company Limited
43 Chowringhee Road
Calcutta 700 071

TATA STEEL

Carrying loads up to 300 tonnes. Travelling 15 km a day. Can you guarantee your crane wheels a longer life?

TISFLOW blanks from Tata Steel

Stronger, longer lasting, more reliable than conventional cast products. And they're cheaper.

Tisflow blanks for cranes, ingot mould cars, gears and trams are made from high quality steel, bottom poured in wide end up moulds, and are closed die forged in a 4,400 ton hydraulic press. The inbuilt quality control measures ensure:
- Fine, uniform grain structure
- Optimum grain flow characteristics
- Excellent response to heat treatment
- Close dimensional accuracy

Tisflow blanks are available in C50, C55, C65 and can be certified to IS:5517. These are also manufactured to meet Inter Plant Standard—Steel Industry IPSS: 1-08-001/1975 Types 500, 630A, 710A and 800A and B.

Table of sizes (in mm)

	Maximum	Minimum
Outer Diameter	875	560
Bore	130	90
Width	235	175
Weight	940 kg	325 kg

For your requirements in these and other sizes and grades, please write to any of our sales offices or to
The Director of Marketing
The Tata Iron and Steel Company Limited
43, Chowringhee Road
Calcutta 700 071
We'll send you the details or have some one call on you.

TATA STEEL

It was during this era that many products were announced – the common strain was the prefix of 'tis' to the name – apparently to associate the then acronym of the company TISCO with the product. There were product advertisements for Tiscral - the water resistant mild steel plate, Tisflow blanks, Tisten - the high tensile micro-alloyed steel, Tistrip, Tisprop and more. The copy was direct and spoke to the industry directly by mentioning technical data, specifications and benefits to the customer.

New dimensions in shape, size and quality...

TIS-BAR FORGE
Tata Steel's Forged Bars
with superior dimensional tolerances.

What makes them so superior?

The products of Tata Steel's newly installed Long Bar Forging Machine have:

1. Closer dimensional tolerances compared to conventional rolling and forging—within 50% and 16%, respectively. Superior tolerances mean lower losses in machining and better yield in precision closed die forging.

2. Superior metallurgical properties achieved due to deeper penetration of the forming force, simultaneous working on the entire cross section and forming in a single heat.

The spectrum:

Shape	Size (mm)	Quality
Rounds	70-250	Plain carbon, alloy and sophisticated tool/die steels through conventional steel making or Vacuum Arc Degassing/ Electroflux Refining processes.
Squares	70-230	
Flats (T=Thick W=Wide)	T: 40 Min W: 240 Max T/W: 1:6 Max	

For your requirements and more details, contact any of our Sales Offices or write to:
The Director of Marketing
The Tata Iron and Steel Company Limited
Tata Centre
43 Chowringhee Road, Calcutta 700 071

TIS-BAR FORGE from Tata Steel's Long Bar Forging Machine for quality, economy and reliability.

TATA STEEL

The high-tensile micro-alloyed steels from Tata Steel

TISTEN

PHYSICAL PROPERTIES (Minimum guaranteed)	MILD STEEL IS:226 Fe 410	TISTEN GRADES				
		TISTEN				
		42	50	52	55	60
Yield Stress N/mm²	250	250	350	350	410	440
Tensile Stress N/mm²	410	415	490	510	540	590
% Elongation	23	23	22	22	20	20
Mandrel diameter for 180° bend: Up to 25 mm thick	3T	2T	2T	2T	2T	2T
Over 25 mm thick	3T	2T	2T	2T	3T	3T

Also available Tisten 52 & Tisten 55 Steels with lower carbon equivalent up to 36mm thickness for improved weldability.

Areas of applications for TISTEN are:
- Cranes, stackers, reclaimers, etc.
- Trucks, dumpers, trailers, ships, wagons, earthmoving equipment, etc.
- Off-shore structures, underground structures in mines and collieries, transmission line towers, etc.
- Large span bridges, conveyor galleries, structural members in buildings, etc.
- Containers, high pressure gas transmission pipelines, large vertical storage tanks, L.P.G. bullets etc.
- Pressed and formed components

TISTEN, a group of high-tensile micro-alloyed steels, has been developed and marketed by Tata Steel for over a decade now. Since the improvement in strength is achieved mainly through grain refinement, these steels are tough, formable and weldable.

Now also available with guaranteed impact values at sub-zero temperatures.

Compared to conventional carbon constructional steels, **TISTEN offers special advantages:**
- Low initial overall cost of material
- Reduction in dead weight, increased payloads
- Lower erection and maintenance costs
- Good formability
- Good weldability
- Superior toughness

For your requirements, please write to any of our sales offices or to:

**Director of Marketing
The Tata Iron and Steel Co Ltd
Tata Centre
43 Chowringhee Road
Calcutta 700 071**

TISTEN High-tensile steels from **TATA STEEL**

TISRING for CTC segments. A cut above the rest.

TISRING stainless steel rings for CTC segments give you the edge. The Tata Steel edge. In performance. In durability. In economy.

The performance edge
Unlike conventional forged or cast rings, CTC segments from TISRING are *forged and rolled* in a numerically controlled Radial Axial Ring Rolling Mill. To give you tighter tolerances, minimum machining loss and a superior metal structure, free from cracks.

The durability edge
The high speed of processing, combining forging and rolling also ensures uniform properties throughout the cross-section for longer life of cutting teeth.

The economy edge
Electrical heating instead of oil-fired heating ensures clean, uniform and speedy heating, thus eliminating chances of contamination. To give you a high quality defect-free product that works out cheaper in the long run.

TISRING is made from prime quality AISI 304 Stainless Steel and rigid quality control is exercised at each stage of manufacture.

So, the next time you need cutting collars for your CTC machines, insist on TISRING. The superior alternative from Tata Steel.

TISRING Precision engineered circular products from **TATA STEEL**

For further details, contact:

Sr. Application Engineer (East)
The Tata Iron and Steel Co Ltd
52 Chowringhee Road
Calcutta 700 071

Addl. Area Manager
The Tata Iron and Steel Co (P) Ltd
C/o. Rural Engineering Co (P) Ltd
Kanchan Road, "Meena Bhaban"
Ulubari
Guwahati 781 007

Sr. Application Engineer (South)
The Tata Iron and Steel Co Ltd
20-J Mahatma Gandhi Road
Bangalore 560 001

The hot fact behind the best cold rolled strips in the country

Fact : To get a quality cold rolled steel strip, you need to start with a good hot rolled steel strip.

That's where TISSTRIP, the hot rolled steel strip from Tata Steel, comes in.

Because :

★ While making the steel for TISSTRIP, a tight control on chemical composition is maintained through computerised checks at frequent intervals.

★ A good surface on the rolled strip is ensured by the use of bottom-poured steel and surface dressing of strip bars that are to be rolled into TISSTRIP.

★ When the strip bars are being reheated prior to rolling into strips, a strict control of the furnace atmosphere is exercised to ensure a very low degree of decarburisation.

★ Spark testing and marking of all coils guarantee grade identity.

★ Backing all this is Tata Steel's legendary reputation for manufacturing quality steels. A reputation based on over 75 years of experience in producing steels to international standards and specifications.

That's why, most cold rerollers and manufacturers specify TISSTRIP, from Tata Steel, than any other hot rolled steel strip.

For further information please contact any of our sales offices or write to:

**The Director of Marketing
The Tata Iron and Steel
Company Limited
Tata Centre, 43 Chowringhee Road
Calcutta 700 071**

Grade		End Uses
TISSTRIP	C-30	High strength strapping strip
TISSTRIP	C-40	Cycle chains
TISSTRIP	C-55	Industrial and motorcycle chains
TISSTRIP	C-70	Springs, washers
TISSTRIP	C-83	Band saws, wood-cutting saws
TISSTRIP	C-98	Hacksaw blades, power saw blades and razor blades
TISSTRIP	120 Cr 35	Power saw blades and razor blades
TISSTRIP	15 Cr 3	Industrial chain rollers
TISSTRIP	50 Cr V4	Compressor Valves & Seals Diaphragm Clutches

TISSTRIP The hot rolled, low alloy,  medium and high carbon steel strips from **TATA STEEL**

Meeting your needs. All under one roof.

Special steels; seamless tubes; commercial and precision welded tubes; ball and roller bearings. And, of course, the usual mild steel sections... we have <u>all</u> you need at Tata Steel. The one-stop shop that caters to diverse needs. Smoothly. Efficiently.

A Company with the comprehensive capability it takes to serve industries as diverse as Transport and Mining. Oil and Defence. Construction and Power.

Where marketing does not end with the sale of its many products.

Where scientists constantly develop newer grades of special steels to meet sophisticated demands.

And design custom-tailored products that save valuable foreign exchange.

Tata Steel. A multi-product Company with a single aim. Your satisfaction.

TATA STEEL
The first and still the foremost

Structural solutions from Tata Steel, blueprint upwards!

As an architect, builder or designer, you know how dimensionally different structural constructions can be. In shape and size.

Tata Steel's Tube Division has had a long-standing association with architects, builders, engineering and construction agencies.

Which has helped in the development of total structural systems to suit individual needs.

Scaffolds, tubular trusses, towers or structures of more complex nature.

We will study your blueprint plans, visit sites, check with you for specific requirements and provide you with total tubular structures, built to suit your requirements.

You can depend on Tata Steel structural systems because they are backed by a wealth of experience and a comprehensive quality control system other manufacturers just cannot match. Quality control that begins from the steel-making stage and results in products comparable with the latest and the best in the world.

Rectangular and Square Hollow Sections are two recent technological breakthroughs. Two wonder building aids used in Tata Steel projects.

And you can be sure of their lasting qualities.

So, if you are in the building business, give us your blueprint.

And we'll take it from there—upwards!

For further details, contact:
The Structural Engineering & Projects Department
The Tata Iron and Steel Company Limited
Tata Centre, 43 Chowringhee Road
Calcutta 700 071
Phones: 29-3861 (10 lines); 29-1981 (10 lines)
Telex: 021-7511, 021-2768

structural systems from **TATA STEEL**

ANOTHER FIRST FROM TATA STEEL

New-generation reinforcing bars for the builders of tomorrow

Progress is a watchword at Tata Steel. This has prompted us to develop India's first Fe-500 rebars, TISCON-50. These bars have a minimum guarantee level that conforms to IS-1786 and meet every necessary parameter demanded by the construction industry. TISCON-50 bars are either cold-twisted or thermo-mechanically treated. Both categories are interchangeable and can be used in tandem.

- Higher saving in steel over Fe-415 bars.
- Can be both butt welded and lap welded with excellent result.
- Superior yield strength—500 N/mm².
  Superior tensile strength—545 N/mm².
- 60% higher bond strength, compared to mild steel.
- Up to 180° angle bendability through 2a for diameters up to 25 mm. Rebendability up to 157.5° angle.

TISCON-50

TATA STEEL
The first and still the foremost

---

121 quality control checks are helping to hold the Indraprastha Indoor Stadium together.

And the Jawaharlal Nehru Stadium, the Talkatora Indoor Pool, the Asiad Village... in fact, all new constructions at the Asian Games Complex.

Because TISCON, from Tata Steel, is the superior ribbed reinforcing bar that more and more architects and engineers, from all over India, are specifying.

The reason? Its quality.

At Tata Steel, quality is carefully built into TISCON at each and every stage of its production. From analysis and monitoring of raw material quality, to controlling and checking chemical compositions at blast furnaces and steel melting shops, to controlling and ensuring conformity to specification at the rolling mills and testing laboratories. In all, 121 quality control checks meticulously monitor and test every aspect of TISCON. The result? A superior ribbed reinforcing bar with consistent properties.

For more information on TISCON bars, write to us at any of our sales offices. We'll send you the details or have someone call on you.

TISCON
The superior ribbed reinforcing bar

TISCON
A 75-year experience in quality control is helping Sri Sailam take the force of over 50 million cubic metres of water.

And the Baira Siul on the Ravi, the Salal on the Chenab, the Batsa in Maharashtra... in fact, all the dams and barrages built in the last decade.

Because TISCON, from Tata Steel, is the superior ribbed reinforcing bar that more and more architects and engineers, from all over India, are specifying.

The reason? Its quality.

Because each of the 300,000 tonnes of TISCON, produced annually, is backed by Tata Steel's 75 years of experience in producing quality steels. An experience that dates back to the early years when Tata Steel rejected, as scrap, any of its products which did not conform to British specifications. An experience that resulted in several of the country's large steel plants adopting many of the quality control measures pioneered by Tata Steel. Today, Tata Steel's quality has become a byword in the Indian steel industry. The result of this experience? A superior ribbed reinforcing bar with consistent properties.

For more information on TISCON bars, write to us at any of our sales offices. We'll send you the details or have someone call on you.

**TISCON
The superior ribbed reinforcing bar**

TATA STEEL

TISCON
400 men, 121 checks and 75 years of experience. That's the quality package that is helping to hold the Oberoi Towers up.

And the Bombay Stock Exchange building, the Bombay Reserve Bank building, the Taj Hotels... in fact, thousands of multistorey structures all across the country.

Because TISCON, from Tata Steel, is the ribbed reinforcing bar that more and more architects and engineers, from all over India, are specifying.

The reason? Its quality.

At Tata Steel, 75 years of experience in quality is built into TISCON at every stage of its production. 121 quality control checks meticulously monitor and check every aspect of TISCON and its production from chemical composition to physical properties and specifications. 400 highly skilled, trained and dedicated experts ensure that the slightest deviation in the instituted practices means a rejection. The result of this singleminded obsession with quality? A superior ribbed reinforcing bar with consistent properties.

For more information on TISCON bars, write to us at any of our sales offices. We'll send you the details or have someone call on you.

**TISCON
The superior ribbed reinforcing bar**

TATA STEEL

The company had announced its ribbed hot rolled reinforcing bars a few years earlier as Tistrong and the cold twisted rebar as Grip Bar. It now announced the new name for the products, Tiscon - the superior ribbed reinforcing bars. Prominent structures which defined the skylines of many cities were used in these testimonial advertisements.

Leprosy isn't as dreadful as you think

"I once had leprosy but I was never a 'leper'"

Today, Ram Kumar is an able-bodied 15-year-old. He has no tell-tale signs, no deformities. Nor has the stigma of leprosy left any psychological scars. "I owe it all to my parents," says Ram Kumar, "I was lucky."

If emotional support is necessary, so is the need for early detection and sustained treatment. In Ram Kumar's case, a pale patch was diagnosed as leprosy in its earliest stage. For the next few years, he underwent a course of medication and therapy. In time, he was pronounced cured. All the while, he was made to go to school, play with friends and lead a normal life.

Says Ram Kumar, "My parents and I knew there was no risk. We had understood that leprosy was like any other disease." And so it was.

Leprosy is completely curable

All it needs is ✦ Early detection ✦ Timely intervention ✦ Sustained treatment ✦ Community support throughout

- Leprosy causes no deformities when detected and treated early. In advanced stages, deformities cannot always be remedied
- Leprosy is the least infectious of all communicable diseases
- Anyone can get leprosy, but most people have a natural immunity
- 30% of newly detected cases are children.

However, leprosy is not hereditary

The first signs

- A pale or red skin patch — smooth, shiny or dry
- Total loss of sensation in the patch
- Loss of hair or lack of sweating in the area
- Tingling or ant-crawling sensation around or near the patch

"If you have leprosy, you have nothing to fear"

19-year-old Malti wanted to marry her college sweetheart. But there was a hitch: her history of leprosy. Her parents decided to tell her future in-laws about it. They talked about the treatment and the cure. They reiterated the fact that Malti was free of the disease and that she could not transmit it to her husband or children. "Don't worry," her mother-in-law interrupted, taking off her gold chain and putting it around Malti's neck, "To us, Malti won't ever be a daughter-in-law, but a daughter."

You too can help drive away the stigma. Encourage leprosy patients, support them, retain them in the mainstream of life. Remind them — and yourself — that they pose no threat to their families and friends.

All you need is an open mind.

The real healing touch must come from you

 TATA STEEL

A joint public service in support of the Government of India's programme for the treatment and control of leprosy.

"While my daughter-in-law continues treatment for leprosy, she continues to care for us."

"How vividly I remember the day! Radha, my daughter-in-law, and I were both in the kitchen when a spot of hot oil fell on Radha's hand. 'Put some ice on it,' I said. 'But it doesn't hurt at all!' she exclaimed. We looked at each other, puzzled at first, then worried. And suddenly, the horrible suspicion struck us — could it be leprosy? Radha rushed out and locked herself in her room. She refused to eat, refused to answer all our pleas and kept sobbing, 'I'll go away, I'll go away,' and nothing I said could convince her otherwise.

"When my son Atul came home, Radha was calmer, but no less frightened. 'The first thing to do is to go to the doctor,' said Atul. 'And I'm quite sure there's nothing to panic about.'

"The doctor confirmed that it was indeed leprosy in its early stages. He also told us that leprosy is completely curable. Meanwhile, he insisted that since Radha's case was non-infectious, she should lead a normal life as wife, mother and housewife while continuing her treatment.

"Today my Radha continues to look after us and the house. And I baby sit when she goes to the doctor. She has already responded to the treatment and I thank God that we wasted no time in seeking medical help. Now I know she'll be completely cured very soon."

Leprosy is completely curable — do not fear it, treat it

- Leprosy causes no deformities when detected and treated early. In advanced stages, deformities cannot always be remedied.
- Leprosy is the least infectious of all communicable diseases.
- Anyone can get leprosy, but most people have a natural immunity.
- 30% of newly detected cases are children. However, leprosy is not hereditary.

The first signs

- A pale or red skin patch — smooth, shiny or dry.
- Total loss of sensation on the patch.
- Loss of hair or lack of sweating in the area.
- Tingling or ant-crawling sensation around or near the patch.

Your support counts

Support the national programme for leprosy treatment and control by making sure your family and friends know the facts about leprosy. Encourage early detection and sustained treatment at Government clinics and hospitals. Help leprosy patients to lead normal lives by ensuring that they retain their place in society.

The real healing touch must come from you

 TATA STEEL

A joint public service in support of the Government of India's programme for treatment and control of leprosy.

For further information, write to: Leprosy Awareness Campaign, C/o UNICEF Information Service, 73 Lodi Estate, New Delhi 110003.

The true identity of the leprosy patient has been concealed for want of community support.

In 1985 the company released a public service campaign in association with the Government for the treatment and control of leprosy.

TISCARE
A quality product from Tata Steel

The destitute women of the bustees in Jamshedpur know somebody cares for them as they are taught to make exquisite toys like this one. And discover through toy-making, carpet weaving and other self-employment avenues, the dignity of earning their own livelihood.

These rehabilitation schemes are but one facet of Tata Steel's Community

Development and Social Welfare Department which has a network of 13 centres and reaches out to more than two lakh persons. Covering areas as diverse as education, health, art and sports. With special emphasis on training of children and Adivasis.

For the people, by the people

Believing that change must come from within, Tata Steel has raised volunteer corps drawn from the community. Known as

the Seva Dal, Mahila Dal and Yuvak Dal, these groups of workers receive training in hygiene, fire-fighting, home economics, good citizenship, etc.

Tiscare has come to mean hope in so many areas. Ranging from health services to sports programmes. Employee welfare to community service. Rural development to relief and rehabilitation. Tiscare means many different things to many different people.

To Tata Steel, it is a continuing commitment to improving the quality of life.

TATA STEEL

TISCARE
A quality product from Tata Steel

Mothers like her receive a special kind of care under the Tata Steel Family Planning Programme implemented through nine Family Welfare Centres and eleven Child Clinics which provide free health care services to a large number of people living in and around Jamshedpur.

The programme covers pre-natal check-ups, immunisation, contraceptive counselling and motivational education programmes for special focus groups. The 'Parents of Tomorrow' programme, for instance, aims at newly married couples between the ages of 18 and 25 years and covers family relationships, health and sex education.

Record achievement

Tata Steel's Family Planning Programme has resulted in Jamshedpur already attaining a birth rate of 19.81 per thousand, targetted for the country as a whole, by 2000 AD, according to the International Institute of Population Sciences. Thus, in this important field, Jamshedpur is already on the threshold of the 21st Century.

Tiscare has come to mean hope in so many areas. Ranging from health services to sports programmes. Employee welfare to community service. Rural development to relief and rehabilitation. Tiscare means many different things to many different people.

To Tata Steel it is a continuing commitment to improving the quality of life.

TATA STEEL

TISCARE
A quality product from Tata Steel

Milch cattle receive special care under animal husbandry programmes organised by the Tata Steel Rural Development Society (TSRDS). Started as a voluntary agency in 1979, TSRDS today covers 120 villages around Jamshedpur and 110 villages in Tata Steel's mines and collieries. People's participation plays a vital role in this ambitious venture that extends beyond animal husbandry to other areas of rural life as well.

Two crops where there was one

TSRDS entered a mono-crop area with very low irrigation facilities. Realising that rabi cultivation could revolutionise rural economy, it undertook field-based training programmes and started demonstration farms.

Today, hundreds of families are reaping second crops, thanks to cash crop cultivation over vast acreages.

Helping people help themselves

Rural industries are encouraged so that traditional skills and craftsmanship may be gainfully employed to augment family incomes. On-going schemes include cane furniture making, cocoon rearing and tussar silk weaving.

Community forestry has also been given an impetus by Tata Steel. A concerted programme of afforestation, through plantation and introduction of new and useful species of plants, has helped turn vast stretches of barren land into green areas.

The rehabilitation of fast-vanishing tribes like the Birhores,

building of link roads and irrigation projects, the supply of clean drinking water, the establishment of schools and health services, are some of the other TSRDS schemes that have helped change the face of rural areas around Jamshedpur.

Tiscare has come to mean hope in so many areas. Ranging from health services to sports programmes. Employee welfare to community service. Rural development to relief and rehabilitation. Tiscare means many different things to many different people.

To Tata Steel, it is a continuing commitment to improving the quality of life.

TATA STEEL

In its commitment to improve the quality of life, Tata Steel launched a social product in 1987. This was Tiscare. The city of Jamshedpur had by then many community development centres which covered various facets of social welfare activities and programmes under the umbrella of education art, sports and health. Tata Tiscare also covered rural development and rural industries. A series of advertisements were released in the general press and in trade journals and special publications.

Fame and Claim

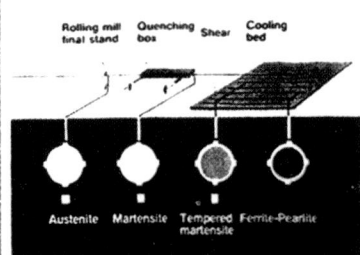

January 1989. The first lot of TISCON TMT bars are rolled at the new 300,000 tpa Bar & Rod Mill of Tata Steel. And once again Tata Steel creates history by introducing India's first thermo-mechanically treated re-inforcing bars.

TISCON TMT is in fact the latest in Tata Steel's long list of 'firsts' that has earned it the fame of a true pioneer.

TISCON and the revolution of the 70s

In the seventies, Tata Steel introduced TISCON, a product of cold twisting technology that helped the construction industry to solve the old 'strength-ductility' problem inherent in the mild steel plain bars.

In TISCON the carbon content was restricted to a minimum level to impart acceptable values of ductility, bendability and weldability, and the bar strength was also dramatically increased.

In many major national projects and in innumerable construction sites, TISCON proved its quality and the quality of Tata Steel technology.

TISCON TMT—The new generation rebar

Today, in step with changing time and technology, Tata Steel announces the beginning of a stronger foothold. Produced by the world's most advanced technology—the 'Tempcore Process'—introduced in India for the first time by Tata Steel under licence from Centre de Recherches Metallurgiques (CRM), Belgium, TISCON TMT offers a unique package of benefits.

The 'Tempcore Process' involves three stages of heat treatment that gives the bar a unique grain structure. It consists of a tough outer layer of tempered martensite and a ductile core of ferrite-pearlite ensuring an excellent combination of strength and ductility.

Better bending and rebending

The tough outer surface and ductile core of TISCON TMT result in a rebar with excellent values of bendability. The bar can be bent and rebent around very small mandrels, offering obvious advantages at construction sites.

Superior weldability

Owing to its low carbon content and low carbon equivalent, TISCON TMT has a weldability which is superior to conventional cold twisted bars. can be butt-welded or lap-welded using ordinary rutile coated electrodes of matching strength. In manual arc welding no pre-warming or post-heat treatment necessary.

Look for this mark to identify a genuine TISCON TMT bar. This is a TISCON TMT 42 bar.

A TISCON TMT 50 bar would carry a 'TT' mark.

India's first and only Thermo-Mechanically Treated reinforcing bar based on TEMPCORE technology.

TISCON TMT

The more challenging the assignment, the

The Modernisation in Eighties

As a part of its modernisation phase the New Bar & Rod Mill was inaugurated in 1987 and the Nation had its first Thermo-Mechanically Treated rebar.

The product Tiscon TMT. Launch advertisements were released in colour and monochrome in major publications and trade journals.

"For us, energy is not an abstract ideal. It is a target for today and tomorrow."

Mr A D Baijal, Divisional Manager, Planning. His comment is in fact a commentary on the philosophy behind TISTECH. A unique emphasis on relevance, result and accountability that marks every action at Tata Steel.

Energy is a major concern for TISTECH, for today and for tomorrow.
And Tata Steel charted out the future, way back in 1928, when an independent Energy & Economy Department was set up.

Because the world is fast running out of energy reserves and the cost of energy is skyrocketing, Tata Steel has taken steps in the right direction. Today, the Tata Steel Plant has the lowest specific energy consumption among steel plants in India.

From raw materials to steel processing, from ancillary units to auxiliary services, Tata Steel has shown the way in effective and relevant energy management.

Creating sinter from blue dust. Using stamp charging technology to convert low grade coal to high grade coke. Using KORF technology to reduce heat working time in OH furnaces. Increasing blast temperatures to conserve coke. Using international technology to solve national problems.

Today, Tata Steel is concentrating on generating captive power. Generating power from washery rejects using Fluidised Bed technique at Jamadoba is merely one example of how Tata Steel is moving towards being a totally self-sufficient and energy-efficient company.

Using Concast as an alternative route to conventional ingot casting, Tata Steel has eliminated an entire stage of energy consumption. By the end of Phase III—Concast will account for over 60% of total production.

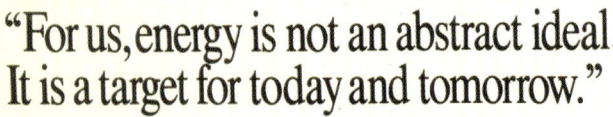

These are targets that convert precepts into practice, ideals into benefits, potential into performance. Because, at Tata Steel, this awareness is felt and shared by everyone. From the miners to the engineers. From the foremen to the executives.

Because TISTECH ENERGY is more than an energy conservation programme in a steel plant. It is a pioneering attempt at evolving a technology that is relevant and an attitude that is contemporary. TISTECH ENERGY is a deep rooted commitment towards meeting the country's needs of today without compromising its tomorrow.

- **Generating 120 MW of captive power by 1990**
- **Eliminating an entire stage of energy consumption through Concast**
- **Reducing specific energy consumption to less than 8.75 G cal/t**
- **Introducing KORF in all open hearth furnaces**
- **Introducing Energy Optimising Furnaces to reduce energy consumption**

TATA STEEL
The first and still the foremost

Recovery and utilisation of waste nitrogen

Stamp Charging in Coke Ovens Battery No. 7

...kes a leader to make global know-how feel at home in India

It takes TISTECH

It takes more than just new technology to carry a country like India into the 21st century. Because even the finest international expertise must match the Indian experience.

Every step of Tata Steel's massive modernisation programme reflects a deep understanding of the country's emerging needs and an ability to innovate the appropriate technology to meet them. While opting for oxygen steelmaking, Tata Steel probed the relevance of experience by specifying the LD vessels which could cope with the high silicon content of Indian steel.

A waste recycling plant with 99.2% efficiency. One of the largest Vacuum Arc Degassing units in the world. The very latest KORF Oxygen Refining Fuel Technology for furnaces. India's first High Speed Single Strand Bar & Rod Mill to introduce thermo-mechanically treated re-bars. The list of successful projects is growing by the day.

The TISCO Direct Reduction Process for manufacture of sponge iron. The Electro-Flux Refining process. The T-Stop slide gate refractory technology, the only one of its kind in India. Identification of stamp charging technology as the most appropriate pre-carbonising technique for low grade coking coal. Tata Steel's R&D programme

Long Bar Forging Control Room

has to its credit a number of significant successes.

A Growth Shop that meets not only the growing equipment needs of the Company but also those of heavy industries in India and abroad.

Along with new generation technology, Tata Steel is investing in the development of a new generation of people. Because any systems integration must first integrate with the people and their practices.

Bar & Rod Mill

The XRF in the LD Lab

And this is how Tata Steel is transforming itself.

Because TISTECH is more than just modern plant and equipment. TISTECH is technology given the experience that spans eight decades. TISTECH is the attitude that masters the challenges of growth and change.

TATA STEEL
The first and still the foremost

Tistech

The adoption and use of technology over the decades coupled with a host of innovations gave birth to a new concept – TISTECH '.. the attitude that masters the challenges of growth and change.'

The Tistech campaign was spread over two campaigns that were released in all major national publications and magazines. The first series was on technology and the second campaign was on energy conservation called Tistech Energy.

JN Tata 150th Birth Anniversary
1839-1989

"When you have to give the lead in action, in ideas—a lead which does not fit in with the very climate of opinion, that is true courage, physical or mental or spiritual, call it what you like, and it is this type of courage and vision that Jamsetji Tata showed."

— Jawaharlal Nehru

Jamsetji Nusserwanji Tata. The man who built more than a steel plant. The man who helped build a Nation that we are proud of today.

Jamsetji strongly believed that political freedom without the economic means to support and sustain it could turn into a cruel delusion. That is why he channelised his entire energy to build an industrial base in a predominantly agrarian country.

Today, celebrating his 150th Birth Anniversary, Tata Steel pays tribute to this thinker, planner, visionary. Today Tata Steel pays tribute to the man who inspired India into self-sufficiency.

TATA STEEL
In remembrance of Jamsetji Nusserwanji Tata.
Born on the 3rd of March, 1839.

Founder's Day

The Founder, Jamsetjee Nusserwanjee Tata, did not live to see his dream: the steel plant and the city of Jamshedpur. However the steel plant was erected and a modern city came to be on the map of India. The dream of the Founder was nurtured to fruition by Dorab Tata, Ratan Tata, R D Tata and J R D Tata who believed in the Founder's vision. This passion to see a strong India with a global presence continues under the present Chairman Ratan N Tata.

On the birth date of the Founder, the 3rd of March, the company releases advertisements each year as homage to this Great Visionary and Son of India.

GONVILLE & CAIUS COLLEGE

JAMSETJI NUSSERWANJI TATA
Founder of the Indian Steel Industry
Born 1839—Died 1904.

"When you have to give the lead in action, in ideas—a lead which does not fit in with the very climate of opinion, that is true courage, and it is this type of courage and vision that Jamsetji Tata showed, and it is right that we should honour his memory and remember him as one of the big founders of modern India."

JAWAHARLAL NEHRU
at the celebration of the Indian Steel Industry's
Golden Jubilee at Jamshedpur in March 1958.

J. N. Tata
3rd March 1839—19th May 1904

A GIANT AMONG MEN

"Jamsetji Tata was a man of great achievement, far-seeing and circumspect. His resolute will enabled him to elaborate projects which his imagination conceived upon the largest scale. He was at once a business man, a patriot, and a thinker, whose service to India was as great as his love for her was profound."

From
Jamsetji Nusserwanji Tata—A Chronicle of His Life
by Frank Harris

tribute to a pathfinder

One of the first Indian ventures in shipping was the Tata Line, started in 1894 by Jamsetji Tata, to ply the India-China-Japan route. The Tata Line survived only a few months and was overwhelmed by powerful foreign competitors, waging a relentless 'war of freights'. Its brief career served, however, to underline the value of a national mercantile marine—an aim towards which no substantial progress could be made until after Independence.

This failure, no less than Jamsetji's enterprises crowned with success, bears testimony to the courage and vision with which he pursued his many schemes to build a new, industrialised India, infused with the spirit of modern science and technology.

Founder's Day/1960

J. N. Tata
March 3, 1839 —
May 19, 1904

The Tata Iron and Steel Company Limited

One of the founders of modern India..."

"Some of our young people are very brave because it is easy to be brave when (there is an) appropriate climate for it. Difficulties come when you are brave by yourself, not in a crowd. When you have to give the lead in action, in ideas — a lead which does not fit in with the climate of opinion — that is true courage...and it is this type of courage and vision that Jamsetji Tata showed and it is right that we should honour his memory and remember him as one of the founders of modern India.

"I have just said that we have our Planning Commissions today, and we have our 5-year Plans...but Jamsetji Tata formed himself into some kind of a Planning Commission and began his own — not 5-year — but a much bigger Plan."

Jawaharlal Nehru, speaking at the Golden Jubilee Celebrations of the Indian Steel Industry at Jamshedpur on 1st March, 1958

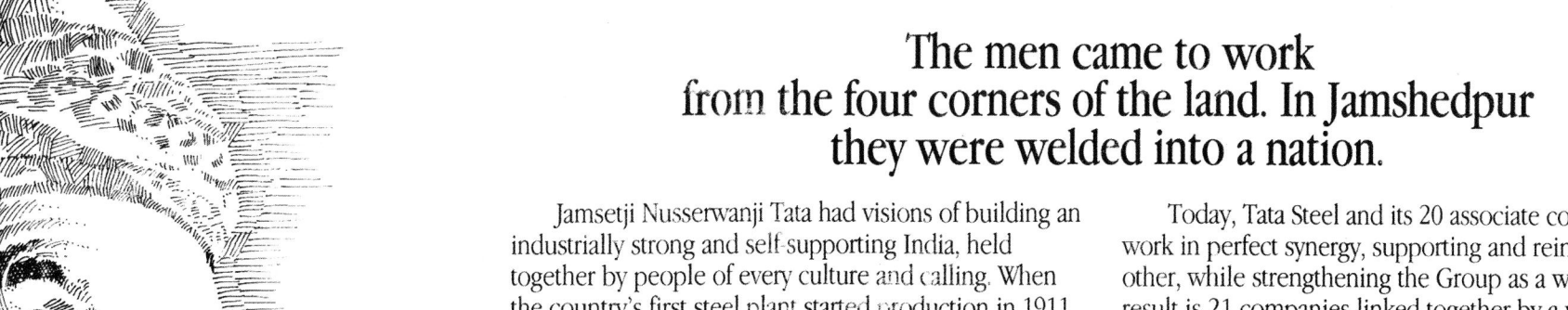

The men came to work from the four corners of the land. In Jamshedpur they were welded into a nation.

Jamsetji Nusserwanji Tata had visions of building an industrially strong and self-supporting India, held together by people of every culture and calling. When the country's first steel plant started production in 1911 in Jamshedpur, Jamsetji's magnificent dream came true.

Founder Jamsetji did not live to see his dream city Jamshedpur or his dream enterprise Tata Steel take shape. But he bequeathed to future generations a legacy of enduring worth : the spirit of harmony and self-reliance.

Today, Tata Steel and its 20 associate companies work in perfect synergy, supporting and reinforcing each other, while strengthening the Group as a whole. The result is 21 companies linked together by a will of steel. The will to build a proud new India with teamwork and confidence, backed by the guiding spirit of the Founder.

TATA STEEL The first and still the foremost

In remembrance of Jamsetji Nusserwanji Tata. Born on this day in 1839.

The freedom-fighters of 1857 pioneered one kind of revolution

Jamsetji Tata masterminded another kind of revolution

He welcomed the struggle for political freedom. But he saw that real freedom meant economic freedom. Alone in his generation, he realised that without steel, power and scientific education and research, no country could be truly free.

The Tata Iron and Steel Works, the hydro-electric projects and the Indian Institute of Science, although completed only after his death, remain as great memorials to **Jamsetji Nusserwanji Tata** —a visionary, realist and revolutionary to whom Tata Steel pays homage on the 129th anniversary of his birth.

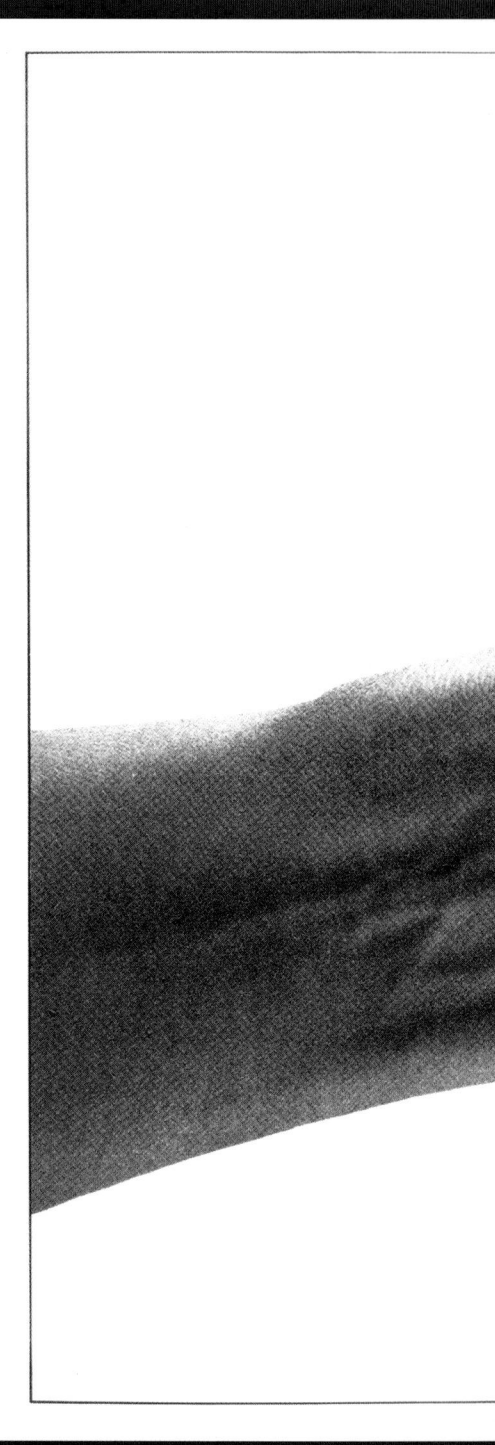

Nineties - The Decade of Exports

Tata Steel declared the 90s as the Decade of Exports. The export department had a clear mandate and apart from steel, the company also undertook the exports of commodities such as pepper, shrimp and coffee. To announce this the agency created a three part campaign with extremely catchy headlines. Cleverly worded, the headlines of these advertisements made steel seem edible!

The legendary television campaign 'We also make Steel' was also launched. This successful series was not adapted for a print campaign. This is, perhaps, one of the most oft recalled television campaign in India.

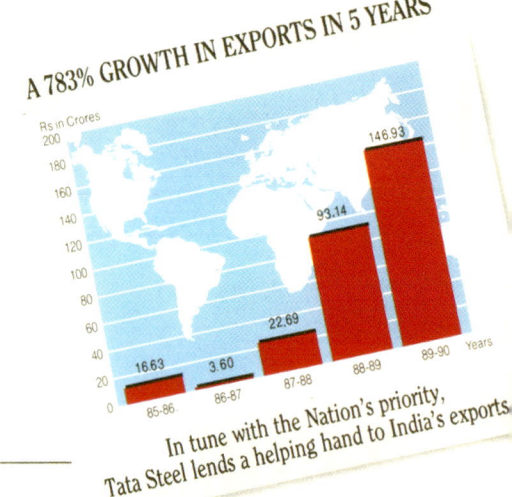

...ouraged the Americans
...le coffee while
...t of steel
...wires

As foreign exchange is a big crunch in India and earning hard currency through exports a national priority, in 1983-84, an eighty year old pioneer decided to move into a field in which it had no major experience.

Six years later, Tata Steel is one of the country's largest exporters with major markets in the USA, Japan, Australia and China and with significant entries into Saudi Arabia, Qatar, Egypt, Turkey, West Germany, Bangladesh, Taiwan, Indonesia, Malaysia and other countries. And, in spite of importing a substantial amount of equipment and raw materials for its on-going modernisation drive, Tata Steel has become a nett exporter. In 1988-89, Tata Steel won the prestigious EEPC shield.

The decade of 90s is the Decade of Exports at Tata Steel. And the pioneer is spreading all its expertise and experience across the seas to build a long term base for Indian products — all over the world.

Tata Steel Exports:

Steel and Steel-based engineering products	Wire rods, re-inforcing bars, structurals, tubes, wires, bars, cranes, rolls, bearings, etc.
Raw Materials	Chrome ore & concentrates, manganese ore, ferro-manganese, ferro-chrome, charge chrome, refractories, etc.
Commodities	Black pepper, coffee, black tiger shrimps

The Chief Marketing Manager, Exports, making a presentation to American buyers

TATA STEEL
DECADE OF EXPORTS
1990   2000

TATA STEEL
The first and still the foremost

Voice of Dissent

The Export Campaign was followed by a corporate campaign that exhorted India to raise the Voice of Dissent as a key to success. The word 'no' was seen as a positive one which could spur changes in a stagnant environment. This was again a novel campaign where the company encouraged India to dissent but with a purpose and reason. This campaign was a series of four and was sketched by the legendary cartoonist R K Laxman.

THE WILL TO WIN

5

"TO STAY ON TOP INNOVATE AT THE BOTTOM"

At Tata Steel, the pace of change is decided not by top management alone but through the Total Team concept – creative solutions shared from the bottom to the top.

Today, responsible decision making by workers is the new way of solving problems at Tata Steel. Networking across levels is creating an environment of innovation, confidence and pride on the shop-floor, in every plant.

And the results? When the state-of-the-art 'G' Blast Furnace was commissioned, it broke all records by producing to capacity within 25 days – a world record. A true tribute to teamwork at Tata Steel, because today, every Tata Steel worker can say with pride, "This plant is mine".

And that is the pride and confidence that reflects the spirit of the New India.

Reflected by the Tata Team and Tata Technology at Tata Steel.

TATA STEEL
THE WILL TO WORK. THE WILL TO WIN.

Will to Win

The television centric campaign 'We Also Make Steel' was a huge success, the wake of which not only set a different style but also triggered campaigns by other corporate houses. In 1993 it was decided to launch a fresh corporate campaign with the theme 'Will to Work - Will to Win'. This campaign, for the decade of globalisation, was created by O&M and released in the general press and journals. A television commercial was also made on this theme.

Speaking of technology someone rightly said, "What is new at dawn is obsolete by dusk".

Which means to stay ahead, know how to select ahead in technology. Choosing technologies that balance excellence with efficiencies. Leaving room for upgradable paths. Developing your own to meet your unique needs.

The Tata Steel Growth Shop for example, demonstrates how the most advanced engineering equipment can actually be fabricated and made available in India.

In keeping with our 24 hours a day, 7 days a week modernisation programme, a whole new generation of technologies is going on-line.

For example, the new one million tonne 'G' Blast Furnace, the advanced slab caster and the one million tonne Hot Strip Mill are integrated together to form a world class, state-of-the-art steel plant. Among other industries, it provides flat products to meet India's automobile, electrical and LPG needs.

This is just one part of what is happening at Tata Steel. A dynamic way of looking at technology, to walk with the world.

A reflection of the spirit of New India.

Reflected by the Tata Team and Tata Technology at Tata Steel.

6

"IT IS NOT HOW MUCH WE MODERNISE BUT HOW MUCH WE MAKE OBSOLETE"

THE WILL TO WORK. THE WILL TO WIN.

THE WILL TO WIN

2

"TO BE A PROUD PATRIOT MAKE YOUR COUNTRY A PROUD CITIZEN OF THE WORLD"

The future belongs to those countries that can compete at a global level. For Tata Steel, it will not be enough to be India's most respected company until we can fly our flag in every country of the world.

Which is why the decade 1990-2000 is our decade of globalisation.

Last year, we generated foreign exchange earnings worth 7,230 million rupees, through exports to countries in every one of the five continents.

A reflection of the belief that 'Made in India' will now be a proud label across the world.

A reflection of the spirit of the new India. Reflected by the Tata Team and Tata Technology at Tata Steel.

TATA STEEL
THE WILL TO WORK. THE WILL TO WIN.

The plant that has grown into many, many trees.

The Tata Steel plant is, indeed, unique. Surrounded as it is by the beautifully laid-out city of Jamshedpur with its tree-lined avenues and parks that reflect the Company's deep commitment to the environment.

A commitment that is reflected in Tata Steel's active efforts to preserve the ecological balance in its environs. Afforestation programmes and reclamation of barren lands have been undertaken in the areas around Jamshedpur and the Company's mines and collieries.

Tata Steel. The Company that believes industry must flourish hand in hand with Nature.

TATA STEEL

Breathing space for all our tomorrows

The quest for a greener earth, cleaner air and purer water is as important to us as the making of steel. For we believe, the future of our business, well-being and the planet depends on protecting and renewing the ecosystem we live in.

At Tata Steel it means converting slag heaps into verdant dunes, creating oxygen plantations through afforestation, consuming the least amount of energy for every tonne of steel produced, adopting environment-friendly technology. Much more remains to be done. But as long as we can think globally and act locally, the world would be saved.

TATA STEEL
The first and still the foremost

Casual releases in many publications continued along with the existing corporate campaigns. These were on the theme of environment and tree plantation.

Other casual advertisements spoke about Change and going global. A one-off release titled 'The eyes of the World are on India' was unique. It asked the reader to fold the advertisement page in a particular manner to reveal a new line!

The press launch for a new product Tiscon CRS - a corrosion resistant rebar - had the look and feel of a corporate campaign. There was an entire series of advertisements for this new product and the copy educated the end user and the intended audience of architects and builders about the hazards of corrosion and the toll it took on concrete structures.

Being the first to believe that the sun is the centre of the solar system was earth-shattering.

Getting others to believe it was epoch-making.

When Nicholas Copernicus put forward his hypothesis that the sun is the centre of the solar system, he bordered on the heretical. Simply because his belief ran contrary to the popular belief that the earth was its centre. But Copernicus' courage of conviction aided by scientific observation saw him emerge triumphant.

Blazing a new trail with TISCON-CRS

In 20th century India, Tata Steel was fighting a different kind of popular misconception. The notion that corrosion caused by saline atmosphere, polluting gases, high rainfall, saline sub-soil and brackish ground water was a problem one had to live with because available solutions were too costly and impractical. But Tata Steel, through painstaking research, proved that there is a better solution to corrosion.

TISCON-CRS —'steeled' to fight corrosion

TISCON-CRS — the first ever corrosion resistant, high strength steel rebar. The revolutionary breakthrough in the world of metallurgy. The result of a unique manufacturing process that gives it corrosion resistant properties at least 1.5 times more than that of ordinary mild steel rebars.

Putting innovation to work

But being the first to break new ground wasn't enough. Staying there was just as vital. Which is just what we did through extensive field trials conducted over a considerable period of time. Making TISCON-CRS the ultimate weapon for engineers and architects to combat corrosion-the unseen destroyer. Empowering them to cut down on maintenance costs and increase the life span of both their buildings and their reputations.

Exploding myths with modern technology

So that generation after generation, there can be only one popular belief. That TISCON-CRS is at the centre of a universe resistant to corrosion!

Beyond breakthroughs

TATA STEEL
The first name and the last word in steel

For more information, contact Tata Steel : **Calcutta,** Phones : 2421778/2422015/2427911, Fax : 033-2421687; **Bombay,** Phones : 2675659/2675945, Fax : 022-2619902; **New Delhi,** Phones : 3342646/3342604, Fax : 011-3343196 **Bangalore,** Phones : 2275570/2274109/2271903, Fax : 080-2272953

You call this unfortunate? They call it home.

Every year, millions of people find themselves on the streets. This Year, they could find a friend. In you. Do give them more than just a thought.

TATA STEEL CEMENT

Issued in the interest of the public by The Tata Iron And Steel Company Limited (Cement Division)

In early 1996 the company inaugurated its Cement Plant in Jamshedpur. The new product was simply called Tata Steel Cement. The launch advertisement and subsequent communication were offbeat and evoked great interest.

With additional Iron and Steel making facilities and a slab caster in place the downstream Hot Strip Mill was inaugurated in the year 1994 and was dedicated to Mr. J R D Tata. The company was now equipped to produce grades of steel that were previously being imported. Work was already underway for the setting up of a cold rolling mill.

> **"There is no half-way house between modern industry and old fashioned industry"**
>
> ~ JRD Tata

The late J.R.D. Tata, captain of Indian industry and mentor to Tata Steel, firmly believed that modern industry should continuously invest in modernization and the latest technologies. To deliver world-class products to its customers.

Tata Steel's 1 million tonnes p.a. Hot Strip Mill being inaugurated today, at Jamshedpur, is dedicated to J.R.D. Tata. And is the fruit of all that he believed in. Today, when the new Hot Strip Mill goes on stream, India will begin manufacture of flat products to international standards of quality.

The world class Hot Strip Mill supplied by Schloemann-Siemag incorporates the state-of-the-art Coil Box, ensuring uniform rolling and superior surface finish to a standard not yet achieved in India.

For the first time, special quality hot rolled coils and sheets, hitherto imported, will be made in India by Tata Steel. And India's pioneering steel plant will continue to preserve and further J.R.D. Tata's vision, while playing a major role in India's industrial development.

TATA STEEL
The first and still the foremost

Initially the company used, in its communication material, lines such as 'The First and Still the Foremost' or 'The First Name and Last Word in Steel' - the end user and the customer were absent as far as the message and copy were concerned.

In the 90s the company incorporated into its creatives the all important customer! A series of advertisements were launched that spoke directly to the customer of Tata Steel and referred to the company as the place 'Where you come first'. An internal campaign highlighting the importance of the customer was also launched.

All other product advertisements released at the time of Tata Pipes, Tiscon CRS, Tata Bearings etc. carried the line 'Where you come first'.

Other product advertisements released at the time of Tata Pipes, Tiscon CRS, Tata Bearings, Tata Rings, etc. also carried the baseline 'Where _you_ come first'.

FILL IN THE BLANKS TO UNRAVEL YOUR MOST PRECIOUS POSSESSION

Yes, it's Mother Nature, your most priceless possession. Without it, you and I would be the endangered species. How do we preserve it?

The first step is awareness. That is why we at Tata Steel set up our village level Van Suraksha Committees that enlighten you about afforestation programmes. We help you raise and nurture your own nurseries and teach others in turn. We encourage you to protect your forests and take pride in the land.

All our new technologies stress on minimising the use of polluting fuels and utilise waste products to further use. Behind every move lies our main concern of preserving your most precious possession. Mother Nature.

TATA STEEL
Where *you* come first

THE ABC OF NATION-BUILDING BEGINS WITH YOU

For us, even a task as Herculean as building a nation appears simple as you become the focus of attention. As simple as learning the alphabet since we begin at the beginning—with the ABC. In our Tata Steel Rural Development Scheme, the TSRDS, there is a concerted emphasis on education at primary and secondary levels.

We also endeavour to make sure you never run out of water for drinking or irrigation, travel over wide roads and sturdy bridges and have access to modern health care.

Besides, in the fields of sports promotion, afforestation, family planning, community and tribal welfare, we have undertaken special programmes that keep your interests in mind. Because if you don't have benefits, we can't succeed in our endeavour to build this nation. An endeavour as complex as any, yet, thanks to you, as simple as ABC!

TATA STEEL
Where *you* come first

A FORMULA THAT KEEPS US AT THE CUTTING EDGE OF TECHNOLOGY

$$TS - U = 0$$

A simple formula, indeed, for expressing complex state-of-the-art technology found at Tata Steel. A formula that unequivocally expresses your indispensability in our life. At Tata Steel, without you, our technological ventures would be futile. Absolutely zero!

For example, what use would our technically superior corrosion resistant steel reinforcing bars be without you to enjoy the fruits of living happily in a house that stands up to the elements? Or what use would they be if they could not protect a bridge which you and your family could cross everyday?

As the 21st century approaches, the efficiency of our scientific ventures and technological innovations can only be judged by the ultimate benefits that accrue to you. Hence the formula that makes high technology at Tata Steel seem so simple. As simple as understanding yourself.

TATA STEEL
Where *you* come first

Unwavering in its commitment for the environment the company announced in 1997, in a one-off advertisement about a green millennium countdown. It targeted the planting of a million trees by 2000. The date was, of course, met.

At the same time a short campaign on afforestation, education and technology was also released.

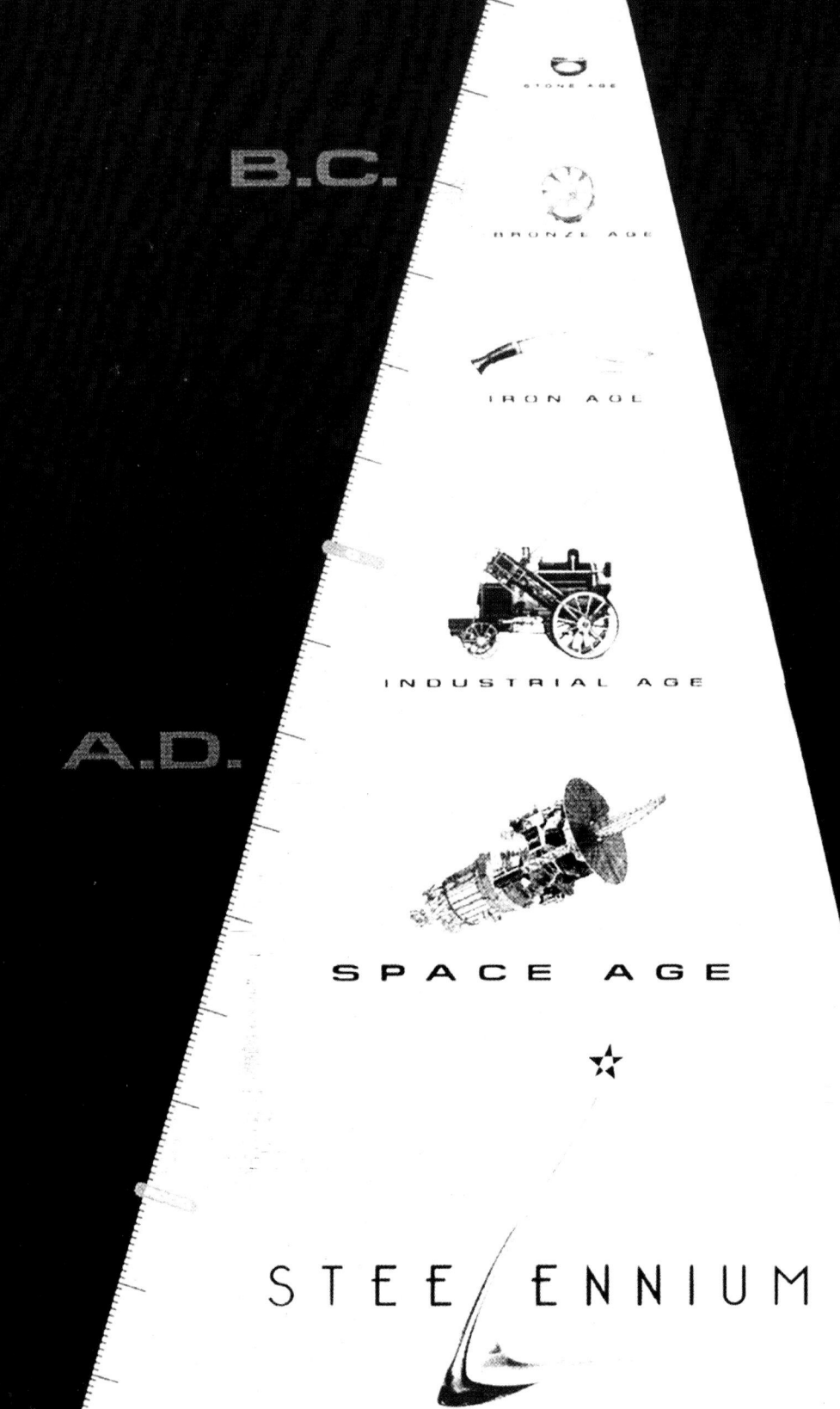

24 APR
TATA STEE
THE F
WITH ITS STATE-OF-THE-ART C

Steel has changed forever. Tata Steel has launched Cold Rolle Strips. Customised to meet not jus the needs of the present day, but o the future as well.

Cold Rolled Strip from Tata Stee is everything you never imagined o steel. Indeed, it is the latest and th most advanced steel of its kind Flexible. Light. Smooth. Precise Lustrous. And what's more, it come in dimensions and thicknesses yo never thought possible.

Tata Steel's **Cold Rolling Mill** ha already created new globa benchmarks in project time an cost. It is equipped with the fines

TATA STEEL

L 2000
UNVEILED
TURE
ROLLING MILL IN JAMSHEDPUR

...chnologies. It provides global quality and delivers at lightning speeds.

...ill it affect our daily lives? Yes. In every way. From cars that will defy ...ne and imagination to refrigerators, ...ashing machines and furniture that ...ill seem like works of art. **Cold ...olled Strip** from Tata Steel will ...ake its presence felt in many ways. ...will affect you in every way – some ...ovious and others not.

...ne thing is evident. The future will ...ot be the same. At Tata Steel, we ...ave christened the future: ...TEELENNIUM. A new age when we ...define steel. And also, ourselves.

...edefining the future

The inauguration of the Cold Rolling Mill in Jamshedpur in 2000 totally changed the product menu. The company was now equipped to meet customer demands from different industries especially the ones associated with auto and white goods segment.

The advertisement was titled '24 April 2000 –Tata Steel Unveiled the Future'. In the copy (re-written by Mr. B Muthuraman!) the company announced that the new name for the future would be Steelenium!

Steel - the inner strength that buildings are founded on. In the shape of rebars, steel sheets, pipes and tubes that resist corrosion and the wear and tear

Inner strength!
Build your world with it.

of time and lengthen the life of the structure. That's reason enough why you should build your world with steel.

TATA STEEL

The Branding Years

With the inauguration of the Cold Rolling Mill the company was ready to cater to the needs of the automobile and the white goods manufacturing sector.

The company was also now ready to consider a radical shift from selling its products as commodities to the marketing of branded products. With systems, processes and the production facilities in hand Tata Steel launched two major brands in 2000. These were Tata Shaktee G C Sheets and Tata Tiscon, the TMT rebar.

Dedicated brand teams were set up in other profit centres and soon the Tata Pipes, Tata Bearings and Tata Agrico were relaunched as brands.

In the following years other product brands were launched. In 2004 the company pioneered Tata Steelium which was the world's first branded cold rolled sheet. In 2005 it re-launched its hollow section business as Tata Structura and its wire business as Tata Wiron.

In 2005 it launched the service brand of Steeljunction and in 2009 it added yet another brand Galvano, which as the name suggests is, galvanised plain sheets.

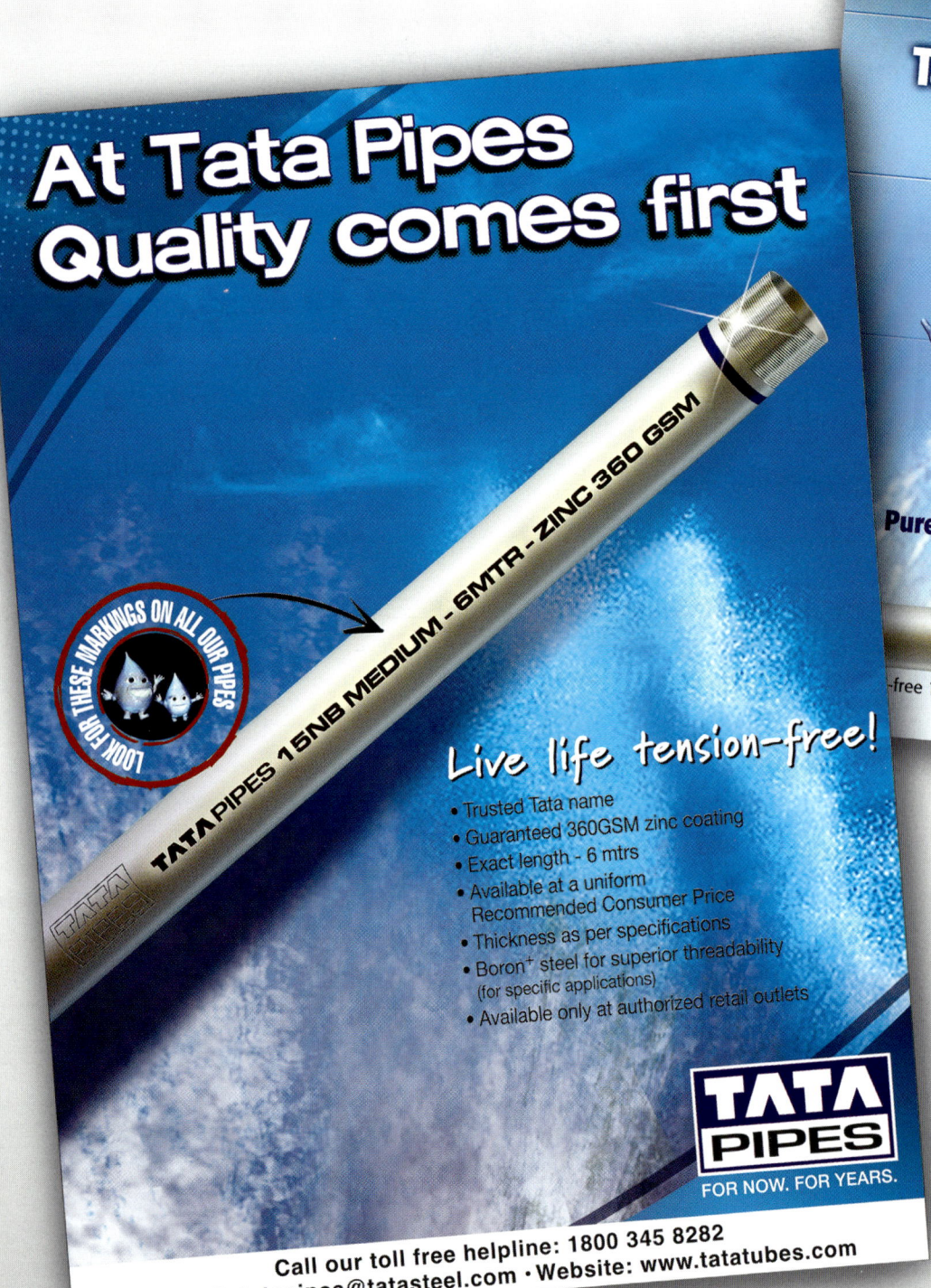

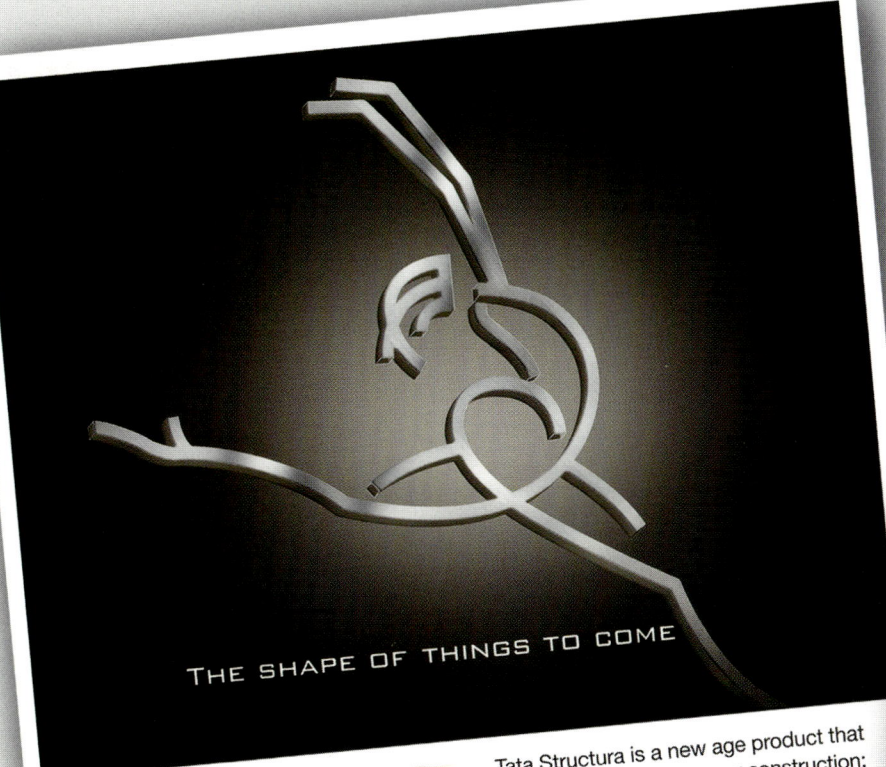

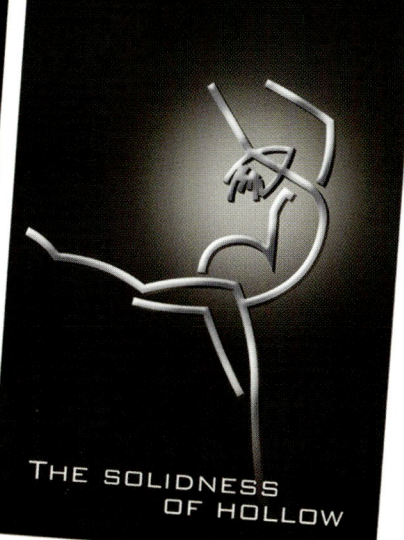
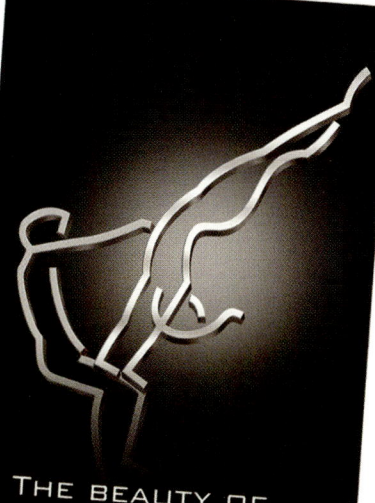

Bearing the mark of Excellence

Tata Bearings continues to enjoy a distinct pride of place as one of India's most valued brands of auto components & bearings. Awards and recognitions provide the reason to excel.

The present product range includes :

- Ball Bearings
- Magneto Bearings
- Double Row Angular Contact Bearings
- Clutch Release Bearings
- Double Row Self Aligning Ball Bearings
- Taper Roller Bearings
- Hub Units

For further information, please visit our website **www.tatabearings.in**

TATA BEARINGS
Happiness depends on little things

Healthy Legs More Eggs

It is easy to recognize a poultry farm that uses TATA Wiron Galvanised Wires. The chickens are not only healthier, but also lay more eggs. Whereas other inferior, rusty wires can hurt the birds' feet leading to lower poultry production. Only TATA Wiron has a uniform zinc coating across its length and breadth, making it rust-free and extremely durable for years together. So if you want the best for your chickens and poultry farm, insist on TATA Wiron.

TATA Wiron — Binding relationships

An enduring relationship is all about understanding diverse needs.

Who else understands your needs better than TATA Wiron? Customized performance, superior quality, international approvals with the latest technology makes TATA Wiron the most trusted name in steel wires. So, Insist on peace of mind. Insist on TATA Wiron Steel Wires only. Get into a relationship that endures for years together.

TATA Wiron — Binding relationships

Tyre Bead Wire | PC Strand Wire | PC Single Wire | PC Spiral Wire | PC 3x3 Ply Wire | WireSpring Wire | Spoke Wire | Ball Bearing Wire | ACSR Wire
Cable Armour Wire | Galvanised Wire | MIG Welding Wire | MS Annealed Wire | Card Clothing Wire | HB Wire | Steel Wool Wire | Tie Wire

100 cc - A Century of Communication

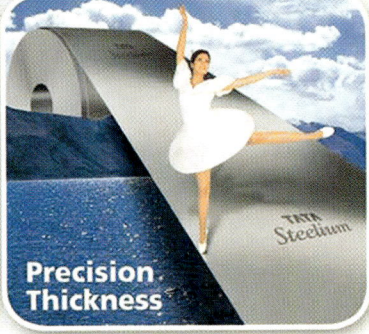

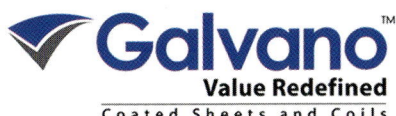

for appliances
Excellent drawability
Absolute flatness
Superior surface texture & finish
Potential for paint cost reduction

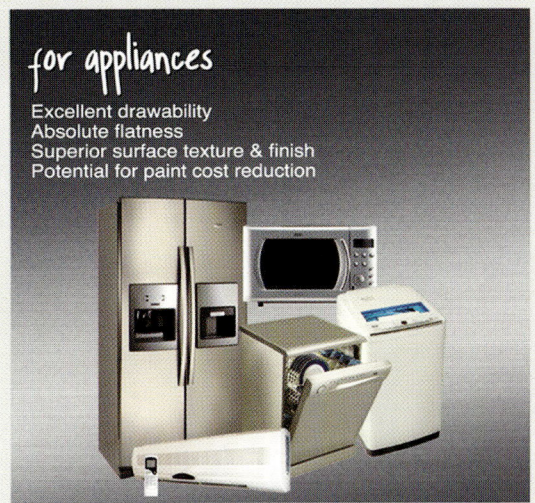

for bus bodies
Wrinkle-free side stretched panel
Absence of drumming effect
Textured surface for better paint adhesion & finish
Improved weldability

for general engineering
Superior surface finish & flatness
Excellent drawability
Enhanced corrosion resistance
Potential for paint cost reduction

for panels
Absolute flatness
Enhanced corrosion resistance
No spring-back effect
Superior paint adhesion

Galvano, as the name suggests, is Galvanised Plain (GP) steel offering available in sheet and coil forms and is set to intensify the reach of Tata Steel further in the steel market. Unlike the ordinary spangled and crushed spangled products available in the market, Galvano is a truly Zero Spangled product with unmatched surface finish and mechanical properties.

A Century of Communication

On 26th of August, 2007 Tata Steel celebrated its centenary.

To sum up its contribution in the last ten decades was a task impossible to communicate either in a campaign or in a single event. To announce its appreciation and gratitude and a renewed pledge towards the nation's progress, Tata Steel released, true to its modest style, a single advertisement to announce the crossing of a milestone that few companies can ever dream of.

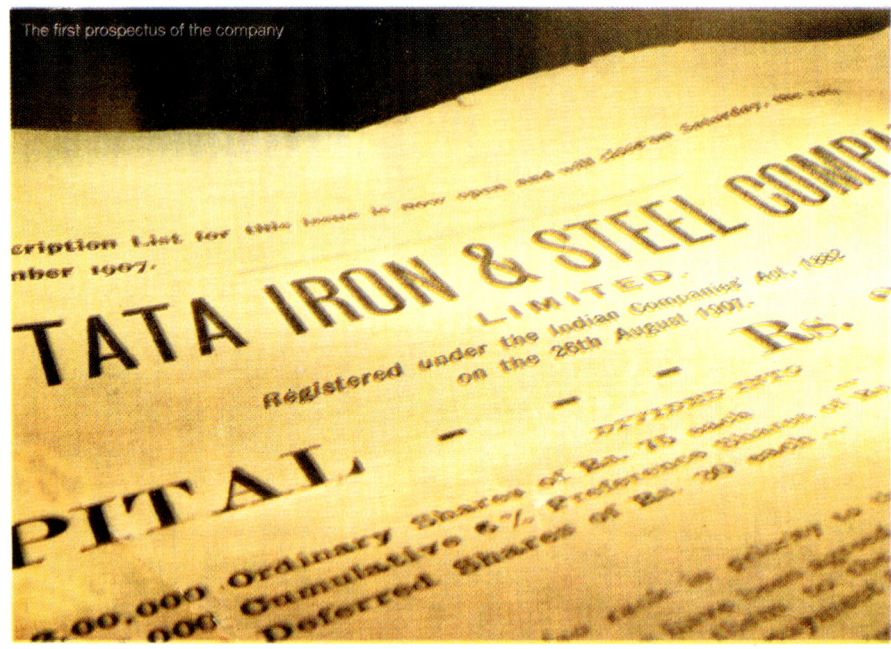

Epilogue

To reiterate, the selection of the print advertisements, reproduced in this book, are from a large repository. There are many campaigns and advertisements that are not featured in this book due to paucity of space. Advertisements that were statutory and routine in nature, such as announcements for share issues, appointments, tenders and financial notices were not considered.

The creations and productions for the electronic and digital media, in the last two decades, are not reflected here. From the first television commercial for the 1988 Olympics and the, oft recalled, We Also make Steel series of 1989, to the recent releases on the electronic, digital, radio and out of home platforms by Tata Steel Brands are also not included. That may be another book!

There were times, while selecting and compiling the advertisements, when one was tempted to write on the progress and status of Tata Steel through the decades. Much could have been written of the turbulent times of the Twenties, the expansion programme and the Indianisation of the management in the thirties, the resolve that the company took in the Forties and Fifties to build a strong and purposeful Nation which continues even today when it has crossed its borders and is a global player.

The book could have been punctuated with anecdotes and statistics, with quotes and production figures, with incidents and plans, with fresh accolades and awards, with new products and successful brand stories but this collection was not conceived with that thought in mind.

This is a tribute to the Creators of the collection.

This is to applaud the effort put in over the years by the advertising agencies, the visualisers and art directors, the copywriters and the production team, the studios and the printers and of course the in-house team at Tata Steel.

There will be more to communicate as the years pass onto another century. Tata Steel will grow and help others grow – as has been its core philosophy – and the need to communicate will be as essential as ever. Technology will ensure different platforms of formal messaging systems – the ones that exist today were figments of imagination just a few decades ago! Yet, in that constant change, the initial thoughts of the early Communicators – to build a Strong Community, for a Strong Nation will forever remain a guiding beacon.

Rajiv Soni
August 2010

References

The Steel Industry of India by William A. Johnson

A Steel Man in India by John L. Keenan

The Making of the Indian Working Class by Vinay Bahl

The House of Tata by Sunil Kumar Sen

Iron and Steel Industry of India by N.R. Srinivasan

India's Legendary Wootz Steel by S. Srinivasan and S. Ranganathan

The Creation of Wealth by R.N. Lala

Tata Steel Archives, Jamshedpur

5